SONG STORY

A Songwriter's Faith Journey *from the*
Jesus Movement *to* Butterfly Kisses

RANDY THOMAS

VIDE

Vide Press
6200 Second Street
Washington D.C. 20011
www.VidePress.com

ISBN: 978-1-954618-33-6

Printed in the United States of America

For Yahweh Tsidkeynu,
Lori,
our family,
and their families.

His mercy extends to those who fear him,
from generation to generation.
(Luke 1:50)

Contents

You Should Write a Book!

For where two or more are gathered in my name,
there am I among them.
(Matthew 18:20)

I PREFER TELLING stories to at least two people at a time. Two people react and laugh more readily than one. Everyone loves a good story. When I recall some of my Sweet Comfort Band adventures, friends say, "You should write a book!" If I tell church friends some ALLIES anecdote, they say, "You should write a book!" The same happens with Shania stories, Dolly Parton stories, and "Butterfly Kisses" stories. I think even my beloved bride said I should write a book. (And she probably tells me that I never listen to her.)

So what did I do?

I spent ten years working on a fantasy fiction novel.

(I'll give you a moment to finish shaking your head.)

The unreleased novel is called *Rain Travelers*. After it grew to over 100,000 words, I thought it was time to shop for a publisher. And do you know what the publishers said? "You should write a book about songwriting!" Harrumph. As a fiction writer, I'm an unknown quantity. But as a songwriter, I guess I'm less of an unknown quantity!

So I prayed. It was tough shelving my previous work. But I learned something: It's a lot easier writing your life story than making up fiction. I was also reminded that

God is writing the story of my life, and it ain't over yet. There's still change in the wind. I stopped harrumphing and began hunkering down to work.

I set up an imaginary movie projector in my brain and started splicing together the highlight reel. I faced a palpable dread that a memoir is an admission that your best days are behind you. That was overcome by the realization that God has blessed me far more than I deserve. (And I deserve nothing.)

Songstory took shape quickly. It took a mere six months to write. That's like forty-two months in dog years. Writing the rough draft was enjoyable. But editing? Yuck. I miss the old tape machines. Editing was more real-world then. I'd wield a razor blade to carve out the unwanted passage and leave it spooled on the floor.

Once I finish this magnum opus, what then? I'll spend the rest of my life promoting it. And I hate promoting. On the plus side, it might be like having a new record out. I pray that *Songstory* is embraced by those it chooses. (Lord, please make it so.) May it resonate among Christians, music fans, songwriters, and folded-arm atheists. (Even an atheist would agree that I'm a highly fortunate fool.)

Typing words on a computer screen involves a frightening amount of guesswork. There's no audience. You write stuff and say, "I guess that'll work." Since I didn't have your input, I wrote it to make God happy. As the runner said in the movie *Chariots of Fire*, "When I run, I feel His pleasure." When I write, I too feel His pleasure. He gives gifts for a reason. May He use *Songstory* for whatever purposes He will. While it's the story of my life, it was all His idea.

I hope you read parts of *Songstory* aloud to a spouse or a friend. I hope that some who read it will sense the presence of Christ with them. It reads better "wherever two or more are gathered." It's written from the heart with an audience of two in mind:

Jesus and you.

So, I Wrote This Book Like a Song

Outside of a dog, a book is man's best friend.
Inside of a dog, it's too dark to read.
(Groucho Marx)

SO, I WROTE this book like a song. I started with a title: *Songstory*. This is my introduction, where I need to set the mood and establish a groove.

If you ask a songwriter, "How do you write a song?", he may give you a blank stare. But if you ask a songwriter how he wrote a *particular* song, he'll tell you a story! Hey, if I had a dime for every time someone asked me how I wrote a song...well, I'd have a bunch of dimes.

Songstory is the writer's room narrative of "Butterfly Kisses," "Why'd You Come In Here Lookin' Like That?" and others. Music of the Jesus Movement, Sweet Comfort Band, and ALLIES come alive again in these pages. *Songstory* is a backstage pass to see how Shania Twain was transformed from nightclub singer to an international star. The songs are the musical signposts along the way.

Beneath the music lies a much deeper story; the unfolding of God's grace. And grace is like a tidal wave; you can't stop it.

Songstory begins in the 1960s and continues today. Back in the day of vinyl records, we used to splice the master mix tapes to create our record sequence. In the same way, the opening salvos of the *Songstory* book are placed out of chronological order in order to draw the reader in before providing context. It's like one of those movies that begins with stuff blowing up before you get to know the characters. (And boy, I've met some characters in my life. If there was a dull moment, I must have missed it.) So let the time-travel-text take you to those departed decades of real bands, big hair, and loud music.

For those inquisitive songwriters who are hoping to gather gleanings, I have included a Songstory Writer Tip at the end of each chapter. I stole this idea from Alice Cooper's book, *Golf Monster,* where he ended the chapters with golfing tips. There are more people writing bad songs than playing bad golf. Probably because golf is expensive.

Music is a universal language. What is its origin? The biblical view is this: A loving Creator has bestowed talents upon His creatures to glorify their maker. We are made in His image and called to be little creators. Creative people, if they are honest, marvel at how lyrics and melodies come to them. I think that's God's grace at work. He loves to see us imitating Him.

Artists want to create something majestic—something beautiful. I believe God often cloaks Himself with beauty. Look at a sunset. It reflects glory. The Invisible God is behind that.

There is a healthy dose of irony and laughter woven into the threads of *Songstory.* Jesus possesses a divine sense of humor! So, while you are reading, remember you are not just laughing with me—you're laughing at me.

I pray that God is honored through this effort. Soli Gloria Deo. He is truly the song and the story behind *Songstory*.

Songstory I

If Butterfly Kisses Is What I'm Remembered For When I'm Dead—I Can Live with That

I don't deserve this award, but I have arthritis and I don't deserve that either.
(Jack Benny)

MY ACCEPTANCE SPEECH was folded neatly inside my tuxedo jacket. We were all having an exceptionally good hair day. A palpable hue of anticipation hung above the buzzing ballroom full of famous faces. My lovely wife Lori and I were seated serenely in the front row. Like we owned the place. Next to us was my songwriting partner Bob Carlisle and his wife Jacque.

Just a few feet beyond us, Dolly Parton glid onto the platform. The spotlight followed her. She waved at Bob and me and giggled. Jerry Seinfeld sauntered behind her. They paused together at the mic. Dolly said brightly, "Well, everybody knows why we're here! It's time to award the Grammy for Country Song of the Year!" A polite and nervous applause followed.

Jerry smiled sarcastically and said, "Yes! And without any further ado…," he opened the golden envelope. His eyes got wide, as if he had been stuck with the check for dinner. "The, uh, winner tonight…"

Dolly read over his shoulder and squealed with delight, "BUTTERFLY KISSES!"

Thunderous applause erupted! The camera zoomed in on nominee Tim McGraw, who smirked a bit before he remembered to smile. Bob gave me a rehearsed look of surprise. We hugged. We kissed our brides. The band played the familiar introduction to our song while spotlights twirled around the room. As we ascended the steps, Bob whispered to me, "You do the talking. I...I just can't."

The speech didn't need to be read. There was so much love in the room, I decided to wing it. My voice rang clear: "Esteemed guests, members of the Academy...," I began. Then I blessed the God of Creation for giving the gift of music; I thanked each and every person we had ever met. I gushed about Ray Ware having managed our careers during the lean years. Reba McIntyre kept smiling up at us, crying. Even Alan Jackson deftly wiped away a joyful tear. As I continued speaking, Cher escorted my mother, brother, and sister onto the platform behind us. Madonna came arm in arm with Bob's mom. I ended with, "...and that's why 'Butterfly Kisses' was a gift from God ... for *all* of us!" The orchestra played our chorus.

Garth Brooks led a standing ovation. As we all posed for photos, I caught a glimpse of a luminous apparition standing behind me. Another stood behind Bob. Were we dreaming? It was our beloved fathers' *ghosts!* They were so proud, they were glowing!

At home, our perfectly behaved children were watching the worldwide telecast in their pajamas. They knew the days of their poverty were over. "Butterfly Kisses" had done what no other song could do! From now on, fathers would dance with their daughters, all the unwanted kittens would have a home, and everyone in the world would love each other.

Okay.

So that is *not* how it happened.

Bob, Jacque, Lori, and I had grown up in southern California. Our smog-filled valley was known as the Inland Empire. It was surrounded by mountains. At least, that's what we were told. When the smog subsided, you could see their majestic outline in the distance. It appeared as if a giant had torn faded crepe paper off the bottom of the horizon in inverted V shapes.

If you drove up into those misty mountains, you would find beautiful Arrowhead Springs. Or you could head east to visit Palm Springs. Out west were Hollywood, Disneyland, and the beaches of Santa Monica. We grew up with Sting Ray bicycles, skateboards, surf music, and transistor radios. It was pretty great.

Bob and Jacque settled into a house that straddled the line between bustling San Bernardino and sleepy Rialto, my hometown. Lori and I had purchased a house in the former orange groves of Redlands, to the south-east. By 1986, we were recording ALLIES records at my home, and we had a number-one country song with Dolly Parton. Our *Long Way from Paradise* record did so well, we felt like our band had hit its stride.

In 1990, we made a bold move: We relocated to historic Franklin, Tennessee. Now we lived in a rural setting where the name Bob was pronounced "Bawb." The name Randy benefitted from an additional syllable (Rayandee), Lori's name was unpronounceable (Lah-ruh), and Jacque's name inexplicably remained intact. The studio was now the rustic Radio Ranch, and the Carlisle and Thomas songwriting desk was a booth at Dotson's restaurant.

There had been twelve years of song-crafting partnership leading up to "Butterfly Kisses." Our motto had been, "We want to write someone's favorite song." We wrote it in 1996. It hit in 1997. That, ladies and gentlemen, is the backstory that brought us to 1998, to New York City, to the Grammys.

New York City. The ambiance swallows you up while it stands aloof, like a steel forest. You feel like an ant in the bottom of a canyon. There's a perpetual sound of a siren in the distance, echoing through man-made monoliths. The smell of pretzels is carried along with diesel fumes. Your breath becomes a little cloud. New York snowflakes tumble from the grey heavens, traversing buildings that scrape the sky, flitting happily toward earth to be crushed under a dirty Yellow Cab tire.

This was it. The Grammys are THE stellar annual event when the entire music industry gathers to pay homage to itself. The February breeze was brisk and insistent. Our hotel was a mere four blocks away from Radio City Music Hall. Four blocks.

So we took a limo.

A limo? In Grammy traffic? Four blocks took forty-five minutes! There were four of us in tuxes and gowns, smelling fragrant: Wisecracking Bob, no-nonsense Jacque, the angelic Lori, and my feckless self.

We arrived late. What a zoo! Once all the designer perfumes converge, the awards crowd smells like a fruit salad. Still, it felt like being on top of the world. Here we saw people who were so much shorter and older than they looked on television. Talk about nervous and excited. "Butterfly Kisses" had been nominated by industry insiders! We had always felt lesser than other artists when it came to Christian awards shows. Now we were in the big league.

Rock stars, preening producers, cutthroat managers, famed engineers, savvy songwriters, and record company weasels circled like sharks. It was party week. They had learned the art of shaking an acquaintance's hand and pretending to listen while scoping the crowd for someone more famous to schmooze.

Producer-of-the-year Don Was was standing nearby me looking dreadlock casual and funky. I said hi. He grinned. "Hi, man. Good to see you!" I think he was assuming he should have known my name. I let the tension ride. Bill Cosby walked by, looking supremely unhappy. Bill had a full entourage, so he was getting used to being escorted by guards.

Gwen Stephani looked bored. (Don't you *hate* these things?) My wife Lori sweetly asked her to sign an autograph for our daughter Crystal. Gwen rolled her eyes and huffed like a twelve-year-old. She reluctantly scrawled something on a Grammy program. (Later, having heard the story, Crystal threw it away.)

Most of the ladies had spent next year's residuals on their gowns. There were plenty of gold, diamonds, and pearls on parade. Some young girls ran up and asked Lori, "Are you Sharon Stone?"

I looked at Lori and thought, "Sharon Stone *wishes.*"

We chatted with an unusually normal-looking lady named Shelly. Maybe she sensed that we might be regular folks with a mortgage, three kids, two cats, and a dog named Elvis. Shelly asked, "Are you nominees?"

Lori said, "Well, my husband and his songwriting partner were nominated."

"Oh! What's your song?"

"Butterfly Kisses."

"Wonderful. I love that."

"And what's yours?"

Silence. Shelly blushed. "Um … the uh, the Meredith Brooks song…" We waited. She leaned forward and whispered, "*B*tch*…"

Oh.

I think she laughed as hard as we did!

Did you know they have "seat fillers" at the Grammys? Yep. Our seats were occupied by hired seat warmers who had held our places to keep the appearance that there are no empty seats at the gala! Just as we got settled in (and the seat fillers were settled out), someone announced our category. What? We just got here!

"And the Grammy for country music Song of the Year goes to ... (envelope shuffling) ... BUTTERFLY KISSES!"

Our wives screamed. Bob and I locked eyeballs. We looked like a calculator right after you press "CLEAR." We had come here to watch someone else win! The two of us must have walked to the podium, because I remember being there. What are we going to say? Fortunately, we had both been on stages for decades; we said something, although I can't remember what!

Then we were quickly escorted by people with clipboards to a back room full of press people. Again, we must have said something, because after we said it, we were whisked away by clipboard people again. They pushed us into a room with photographers. They grabbed our hands and placed gramophones into them. A thousand photographers took photos.

And then, I guess they were done with us. NEXT! A clipboard man came up and tugged at the award in my hand. Strengthening my grip on the trophy, I offered him the continued use of his arm if he would back away slowly. He rolled his eyes. "This isn't yours, darling! These are props. The academy will mail you *your* Grammy—the one with your name on it." I looked at the blank prop. I regretfully surrendered it, like Sam Spade handing over the Maltese Falcon to the fat man. (A genuine Grammy is custom made under strict armed Rabbinic supervision and couriered by flying monkeys to the winner's mansion.)

Bob and I were escorted through some backstage areas. We were being bounced from the media beehive. We were deposited in a deserted crimson hallway. And just like that, it was over. Like a car crash. Did that just happen?

We made it back to our wives as Grammy winners who were Grammy-less! (It's better that way. Knowing me, I might have left mine under my theatre seat, by an empty popcorn bag.) Two more seat fillers had to be ejected. Again. Bye. Sorry.

The show went on. (I'm not sure why that was necessary, since we had already won.) A shirtless guy with "Soy Bomb" emblazoned on his chest danced next to Bob Dylan as he sang. He was carried off, but his gyrations continued, as if he were the Energizer Bunny.

The last award was the Record of the Year. The winner was Shawn Colvin. Lori whispered, "I love her!"

A guy swaggered down the center aisle in a long red coat and took the microphone. It was Ol' Dirty B@st@rd. (That's a stage name. He picked that.) He said something about "I went and bought an outfit that cost me a lot of money today, 'cause I figured that Wu-Tang is going to win. Wu-Tang Clan is for the children."

A giant question mark hung over the crowd. Apparently, O.D.B. was a sore loser. (Cut to commercial.) He ruined Shawn Colvin's moment.

We spent the rest of the evening hanging out with celebrities and shaking our heads in disbelief. This was a night that needed no tomorrow.

Morning arrived unscheduled. Lori and I went out and bought our first wireless cellular battery-operated traveling telephone. Lori figured my music career might amount to something after all, and we might need it. I also purchased a ridiculously expensive NBC News hat from the hotel room. It was like my New York Thinking Cap. I put it on and thought of all the cool things I *should* have said the night before.

Flying home from New York to Nashville, we had no Grammy. But we had a phone. *And* I got a ball cap out of the deal!

Songstory Writer Tip: Here are the top ten tips on How to Write a Bad Song:

10. Make it easy! Copy someone else's song!
9. If John Lennon can write a song using one chord, so can you!
8. Who needs a chorus? Write twenty-seven verses!
7. Compose a song about how life sucks and call it "Misty Rainbow Clouds of My Heart"!
6. Make it obvious that you needed a rhyme! Jesus rhymes with pleases; God rhymes with fraud; Holy Spirit rhymes with "so we hear it"! Writing country? Rhyme gone with alone. See how easy this is?
5. Use clichés that are as old as the hills—like they're going out of style!
4. Don't worry if your melody doesn't fit your chords!

3. Spend thirty-two minutes introducing your song! People love that!
2. Don't have a point!

And the number-one top tip for writing a really bad song is:

1. Ignore what the experts say! *If you think it's great, that's all that matters!* Thank you! Goodnight!

Songstory II

Why'd You Waltz in Here Lookin' Like That?

Surprise is God's way of saying "hello."
The response is optional.
(Joan Chittister)

THE LITTLE BLUE house had been hand-built in 1946. It still stood strong against the Santa Ana winds. A red 1966 Chevy pickup pulled into the driveway next to a '56 Chevy. This wasn't the '60s, though. This was 1985. In those California days we had bleached jeans, sleeveless shirts, and very large hair. Bob Carlisle bounded out onto the cracked sidewalk.

"Do you think you could write country with me?"

By this point, Bob and I had had a few number-one Christian songs. We were freshly committed to rebuilding our band's popularity and being songwriting partners. Country music was really taking off. It was actually cool. They were twanging story songs about everything from God to drinking. (Warms a Presbyterian's heart.)

Did I think I could write country? I had grown up listening to Hank Williams, Hank Snow, Patsy Cline, and Buck Owens. It was a rich well of influences. Garth Brooks was ratcheting country up to a whole new level. What had been small-town, white-trash music now played in stadiums and arenas. It was pedal steel and fiddle with rock production. Having no idea what a pivotal moment this was, I said, "Yeah. I think I could do it." Bob started singing me an opening line while slapping a backbeat on his thigh: "Why'd you come in here lookin' like that? Nana nana nanana na … that's the chorus!"

"I love it. What's the verse?"

"Here comes my baby … na na na na na!" This was classic Bob. A burst of inspiration, complete with groove, attitude, and arrangement ideas. All we needed was the story—which is kind of important in country music.

"Cool! Leave it with me. I'll see if I can write some lyrics that are as good as the music!" Looking back, it's hard to understand where the audacity came from. It probably was brought on by the grace of God (Philippians 4:13).

A few days later, we were flying out of Ontario, California, on a long flight. I had a window seat and a yellow legal pad. I had the opening, *"Here comes my baby…"* now what? "She's comin' 'round the bend"? No. That sounds like "She'll be ridin' six white horses." *Here comes my baby … lookin'* mighty fine? No. But I like the whine of a word like "fine" … then the doubts crept in.

I distinctly remember thinking, "What business do I have writing a country song? I'm an imposter. A charlatan. I'm a mullet-haired, non-beer-drinking, non-smoking Yankee who drives a Honda in the suburbs!" There was a good chance that my lyrics would be a pale parody of country, like a bad southern drawl.

Then I recalled some of the swampy themes that John Fogarty wrote about: "Born on a Bayou." "Proud Mary." Yep. Fogarty was dodging the Viet Cong through the San Francisco bayous from a bedroom jungle in El Cerrito! *Play acting.* Similarly, I needed to play act at being a good ol' Okie sodbuster boy from the backwoods of United Airlines seat 19A.

I got it: *Here comes my baby; draggin' my heart behind.* Ooh, "baby" rhymes well with "crazy"—that's a bona fide country song word....

And so it went. When I showed it to Bob, he recognized that we had something big. He clarified two things—the word "here" was to be pronounced "h'yar," and the word "dancin' " would be sometimes substituted with "waltzin'. " Now we had the cherry on top.

We recorded a honky tonkin' 24-track demo in the country setting of my California suburban garage. At least it was *Southern* California. Bob and I recorded drum machine, bass, and guitars. Bob's vocals were great, as always, although more Sammy Hagar than Dwight Yoakum.

Now what? I happened to play the 1/2-inch tape for Benny Hester. He claimed he could get it heard by some major artists. Why not? I made Benny a cassette. That $2.00 cassette was the best two bucks I ever gambled.

Bob and I started to get some phone calls about our ALLIES record, *Long Way from Paradise.* It was selling so well, we were going to receive artist royalties! (An incredibly rare event in Christian music circles, called "recoupment"!) We had two number-one singles, and we were flying high. What could be better than that?

Word Music in Nashville called my house. Bob and I were recording in the garage, so Lori took the call. Lori ran in saying that Dolly Parton had recorded "Why'd You Come In Here Lookin' Like That?" *Recorded.* Past tense. What? Is this really happening? Bob decided we could knock off early that day. As Bob backed away in his truck, he yelled out, "Someday, Randy Thomas, we're gonna be fartin' through SILK!"

We met Dolly backstage before her show in San Diego. We took photos. Then Dolly waltzed into the spotlight and played her hits for ninety minutes straight. After the classic "Jolene," she lit into "Why'd You Come In Here Lookin' Like That?" as her hot new single. Unreal. She finished the night with "I Will Always Love You"—which is one of the greatest ballads of all time. Our song was running with the big dogs!

By the way, Dolly's producer, Ricky Skaggs, copied our demo note for note. The song has some embedded bluegrass influences, and Ricky knows a little somethin' 'bout that. Dolly sang my plane-ride lyrics word for word. She sang the song on Letterman, *The Tonight Show*, and all the major shows. She promoted the song and rode it like a rocket to number one. Thank you, Dolly.

We got to see Dolly a few times. She always had fabulous hair. When I complimented her on it, she said, "Well, thank you, Randy. It sure cost enough!" Of course, the most obvious things about Dolly just jump out at you. It's hard not to stare at them. (When I say this, I'm holding both of my hands out in front of me.)

Yep: Dolly Parton has beautiful hands.

Trucks were rolling by a Holiday Inn café somewhere in Indiana. Two long-haired musicians sat at a table that had a napkin folded up under one leg to keep it from rocking. The bar next door was just opening up. Someone put a quarter in the jukebox. The empty bar came alive with the sound of Dolly's new hit: a song by Bob Carlisle and Randy Thomas. Our song. Nobody at that little restaurant knew us. If we would have told the truckers nearby, they wouldn't have believed us.

We had written a tune that was reaching into every part of America and beyond. I buttered some stale raisin toast. Bob looked at me over his eggs, took a sip of bad coffee, and saluted me with it, saying, "We ... (sniff) ... have arrived."

Five years later, there was a Presbyterian rain falling on the old town square in Columbia, Tennessee. The windows of one building glowed with a warm light. Three Nashville songwriters were showcasing their songs that night to a mass of music fans. I was one of those writers.

Of all the corner cafés in all the world, Phil Everly (of the legendary Everly Brothers) walked into this corner café. I'd had the honor of meeting Phil a time or three. While I was singing, "Why'd You Come In Here Lookin' Like That?", a horrible realization seized me: "Here comes my baby" is the same melody as "There goes my baby"—which opens the Everly Brothers hit, "Bye Bye Love."

When we finished the round, I waltzed over to Phil's table. He was having his customary red wine. Phil said, "We should write a song together!" I was afraid he wouldn't feel that way after my confession. I sang the opening of the Dolly song, and then the opening of the Everly's hit. It was a direct rip off. I apologized that Bob and I had stolen the opening of that legendary 1957 song.

Phil waved his hand. "I won't tell anybody you ripped it off. It doesn't bother me a bit!"

"Really, Phil? You mean that?"

"Yep ... I didn't write it!"

Songstory Writer Tip: Try play-acting in a song. Who says you can't write a bluegrass song? Or reggae? If you always write serious material, perhaps you need to make fun of yourself. The people who say, "You have to write from your heart" either don't have a hit song, or they can write only one song. The song from their heart.

Make stuff up. It can be easy. It can be fun. Know your limitations, of course. You don't see me writing rap songs. Not with a straight face.

Songstory III

Shania Twain
(You Had Me at Mutt Lange)

Seek first his kingdom and his righteousness,
and all these things will be given to you as well.
(Matthew 6:33)

IN THE 1990s, country music more than doubled its
market share. Music Row became the Land of a Million
Music Publishers. Most publishers had a girl in the front
whose job was to keep you from meeting the jaded guy
in the back with his boots up on a desk by a window that
overlooked an alley whose job it was to turn down songwriters. I don't mean the alley had a job turning down
songwriters—the jaded guy was just always looking
out the window as if he were waiting for someone *other*
than you.

In 1995, Gordon Kennedy recommended me to
PolyGram music. I played them about twenty of my fifty
songs. They signed me right up. I started writing feverishly.* The money was modest. It's really "spec" money:

---

* One should never write songs while feverish. Unless hallucinat-
ing loosens things up. Seriously, though, if I had it to do over again
I would not write a song a week. I was very productive, sure. I can
write a pretty good song once a week, 52 weeks a year. So what?
Pretty good songs aren't hits.

They spec you to pay it back. Then they spec you to make them a profit.

I would need a side gig. I prayed. My drummer buddy Brian Fullen called the studio.

I said, "Hey, Brainj!"

"Hey an' all an' everthang! I want to set you up to audition for Shania Twain."

Shania had done a tour with Toby Keith, but not much had come of it. Her sales were in the 40,000 range. So I said, "Hm. Why would you want me to do that?"

"Well, she has a new record coming out. It'll be called *The Woman in Me*. And man—her producer is *Mutt Lange!*"

Brian went on to describe the romance between Mutt and Shania. It was a cute story. They were getting married while making a record. Brian kept selling me on it. He had toured with Shania, and he believed in her. I said, "OK, you can stop now. You had me at Mutt Lange!"

Mutt had produced The Cars, Def Leppard, AC/DC, Foreigner, and the list goes on. I first noticed him as a writer and producer on the album *Lovin' Every Minute of It* by Loverboy. He was a genius at producing artists. He was also famous for not being famous. Few pictures existed of him. Nobody knew what he looked like.

I got a CD from Twain Zone Productions. An audition date was set. The only problem was that I had never done an audition in my life. How would I prepare? The songs sounded like Def Leppard meets Patsy Cline. I charted the songs and learned the guitar parts, the bass parts, and all the harmonies. I learned them forward and sideways.

Lori and I prayed about it. God provides. Matthew 6:33 says to "seek first his kingdom and his righteousness, and all these things will be given to you as well."

The audition was at Studio Instrument Rental (SIR) in Nashville. It was a very cold day, as I remember. When I entered the over-sized rehearsal space, I met Sherry Thorn. She was Shania's assistant. She was also married to the bassist for the Christian band Whiteheart, so we both sort of knew, "Aha, a fellow Christian."

Let me take a sidebar here. When I was a young Christian, I was told that I needed to only play music for the Lord. If I ever went "secular," I would get sucked into a dark vortex and wind up serving the Devil.

I'm very grateful for the many years I spent playing in churches with Christian bands, but the general market music world is not necessarily depravity gone wild. The people you come in contact with can be professional, courteous, and on some occasions, Christians. There. I said it. We now return you to that winter day in 1994 at SIR.

Shania was what you would expect: pretty, Canadian, a great singer, and a very sweet lady. Mutt was not what you'd expect: ruddy face, hair like a cocker spaniel, South African accent, and the nicest guy you'd ever want to meet. (I had heard he was a dictatorial studio tyrant.) After pleasantries, we ran through a few songs. Things went well. Then came the curve balls: Mutt asked me to switch vocal parts. No worries. Mutt asked me to play songs from *The Woman in Me* in a purely accompaniment style, unlike the record. No worries. They put me though an obstacle course of performance scenarios.

When it was over, Sherry walked me down the hallway. I overheard Mutt saying, "Randy's a nice fellow, isn't he? Great player; good singer."

Wow. Mutt Lange gave me three compliments in one breath. I can die now.

Sherry said, "Randy, I need two things: your passport number and your social security number."

"Really? What about the other people auditioning?"

"Well, I saw you play with ALLIES. And Brian Fullen recommended you! Mutt loved you, Eileen loved you, so..."

"Who is Eileen?"

"Oh. Eileen is Shania's birth name." This was inside information at the time. Apparently, I was in. Sherry treated me well from day one. How many others auditioned? I'll never know. But backing Shania without the benefit of a band required a subtle artistic ability; you had to play guitar confidently in the pocket, while singing loose and behind the beat. I was grateful for my experience backing up great singers. The Lord prepares the called.

I had never done promotional dates before. This means anything from singing in a radio station to playing in front of television audiences. One of the first trips took us to London and Glasgow. The other guitarist, Stu (not his real name), was fresh off a tour with the Beach

Boys. Stu had just spent years playing loose and casual surf music. In rehearsal, Mutt started correcting Stu left and right. Once we were alone, Stu showed his irritation: "Hey, what's the deal with Mutt?"

I had done my homework, so I guess I expected Stu to do his. I opined, "Mutt's a perfectionist. He expects you to be note perfect. If you are, he'll leave you alone."

"Yeah? Well, this is the *first time* someone expected me to be note perfect." And that was the last time I saw Stu.

On another international trip, I had a rendezvous with keyboardist Eric Lambier at the London airport. He flew in from Canada. An old friend of Shania, Eric had been blind from childhood. We were Shania's new backup team. We were deposited at a hotel. I guided Eric to his room. He counted the steps from the elevator. Eric then left a keyboard and luggage on the floor of his room. Leaving the door ajar, he asked me to show him where my room was, counting steps. After I showed him, I said, "We'd better hurry back to your room where you left the door open. We don't want someone to rob you *blind!*"

Eric winced. "So to speak?"

I used to lead Eric around and talk loudly at him, as if he were deaf. He would hit me with his cane and yell, "Blind! Not deaf!" He liked to flirt with girls. After flirting he would ask me, "What did she look like? Was she pretty?"

I would answer, "What's the difference? Have you looked in the mirror lately? *You're blind!*"

We did lots of promotional dates on Canadian TV shows, promoting *The Woman in Me*. One show was *Rita and Friends*. I hadn't packed a guitar strap. Shania offered hers. It was in the hotel room, a short walk away. She gave me her key card. When I returned to the sound stage, I strapped on my old Martin. I walked onto a brightly lit platform, surrounded by cameras, and a half dozen mics aimed at us. I was thinking, *I have Shania Twain's hotel room keycard…. Hmmm … I should probably pick a less public time and place to return it…*

To my horror, Shania said over her mic, "Hey, Randy, could I have the key to my room, please?" I hung my head under the lights and returned the hotel card like a mute. (I hope my wife doesn't read this chapter.)

There were some TV shows where we did lip-sync. That really felt wrong. I was holding an acoustic guitar, while the track played electric guitars. I mimed the backing vocals while Mutt was watching us. (Mutt sang the actual vocals!) I was paid to be a prop. It felt funny being paid to fake it.

Well, not funny enough to refuse the money…

Most trips with Shania involved a new guitarist or keyboardist. I was a mainstay. Mutt joined us on most jaunts. On one trip, Mutt flew off to write a song with Brian Adams for the movie *Don Juan DeMarco*. They came up with "Have You Ever Really Loved a Woman?" If you have heard this song, you should be astounded that the song was commissioned. It is brilliant.

When Mutt was elsewhere, Shania's manager, Mary Bailey, would join us. At one lunch, Mary admitted, "I've been so worried that things aren't moving fast enough."

I asked, "Why?"

Mary whispered, "Shania is twenty-seven!" (Twenty-seven was an age when most music careers were over.)

Mutt had jump-started Shania's late launch. Mary admitted, "When Mutt first called, I didn't know who he was. I answered the phone, and some fellow says his name is 'Mutt'! That doesn't sound very impressive, does it? He said he had seen Shania's video, and he wanted to work with her. Randy, I almost didn't give Shania the message!"

Shania had an odd reaction, too. "When Mary told me that a Mutt called, I thought it couldn't be Mutt Lange! Why would he want to work with me?"

Mary laughed. "That Mutt character kept calling! And when the two of them began talking, they also began really liking each other." The "like" grew into love.

Mary told me an astonishing fact: When they negotiated Shania's record deal, Mercury Records' publishing division passed on owning any Shania Twain songs. They didn't think it would be important. Who was Mercury's publishing arm? Why, that would be PolyGram Music! My publisher! The more I found out about the inner workings of the Mutt and Shania business, the more fascinating it became.

While in Nashville, PolyGram executives asked me about performing with Shania. The conversation went something like this:

"You're touring with Shania Twain? Can she sing? I heard she can't sing."

"You heard wrong. She can sing. She's actually amazing."

"Really? Well, we don't expect this record to sell."

"What? The record is great! And Mutt Lange produced it..."

"Exactly. It's not country. And do you know why it won't sell?

"Uh, no. Tell me why..."

"Because she's too pretty. Look at what's selling in country—Reba and Trisha. The secret to selling records with women is to not to be a woman who is threatening to women. Reba looks like a mouse. Trisha has a weight problem. Women relate to them. Shania is just too pretty. Looks like you hitched your wagon to a falling star."

The "falling star" was about to sell twenty million units of *The Woman in Me*. This was not the first or last time I witnessed executives in the music business be smugly and precisely wrong.

I was on stage with Shania when she was awarded her first platinum plaque. The Mercury executives were all smiles and saying, "We knew you'd be a hit!"

But, wait. It gets better. About two years later, we were celebrating "Butterfly Kisses" in New York City. Clive Calder was a smiley music mogul who had a hand in my success. He had 5.8 billion reasons to smile. He also happened to own Zomba Music, and his best friend was ... wait for it ... Mutt Lange! He also shared that beautiful South African accent.

Clive took me to a corner of the room and ran down the Shania and Mutt deal: Mutt had gone to Nashville to ask Mercury for a higher budget for Shania's record. Mercury execs looked at her sales and said no. So, Clive called a major guy at Mercury. Clive recounted the conversation like this:

"Do you know who Mutt Lange is?"

"*Not really. I hear he does rock 'n' roll. This here's Nashville.*"

"OK, look, can you come up on the budget?"

"*No.*"

"All right. How about this: Mutt will pay for half of the budget. He will even pay for half of marketing and promotion." (This got the guy's attention.) "But you will be partners with Mutt Lange on this record. Mercury will only have to shell out for half of the risk dollars. In exchange, Mutt Lange owns half the masters."

(Pause.) "*We can do that.*"

The deal was done. To save themselves a hundred thousand dollars or so, Mercury gave away multiple millions on over thirty-five million units sold. This was likely the deal of the century. For the artist. And the producer.

Clive continued, "So, on thirty million records (seventy million worldwide), the producer's points go to Mutt. Artist points go to Shania. Half the publishing income goes to Mutt. The other half goes to Shania. Half of the record company profits go to Mutt Lange. Oh! Shania will make millions on tour. Let's see. Did I leave anything out? Songwriting royalties go to ... oh, that's right—Mutt and Shania…." Clive called out (in case any Mercury or PolyGram people were listening): "Oh, and by the way, Mutt and Shania are MARRIED!"

Footnote: The Shania catalog now belongs to Universal, who also owns "Butterfly Kisses." Will the irony never end?

Back to Shania tour dates. We played in London at a club called Venom. Not a name I would have picked. By now we had added a whole band, including New York guitarist David Malachowski. The band was given an afternoon off. We were near Piccadilly Circus on West End.

I suggested, "Let's go over to Abbey Road!" I pictured four of us crossing the crosswalk like the Beatles.

The young players blinked back at me. "What? Why? What's that? No. Let's go shopping."

My eyes rolled like a slot machine. David said, "I'll go!" A London cabbie took a photo of the two of us crossing Abbey Road.

That night, Shania told the audience, "I was riding a horse bareback a few days ago while filming a video." She lifted her long dress to show her ankles. They were bruised. "The bruises go up between my knees." She lifted her dress.

The band began to feel uncomfortable. Shania continued, "They go all the way up my thighs!"

David and I looked at each other. He whispered, "Maybe you should start the next song…" The next few seconds seemed like hours.

Then Shania realized she hadn't thought out where this was going. She added, "But I'm not going to show you that." Thankfully, I got the cue to kick off another song. Whew.

Most major artists have a musical director. This is a band leader who can handle the musical (and emotional) details so that the star walks on stage with peace of mind. Shania was her own MD. She ran rehearsals. One day, Shania said to me, "Randy, I like how you don't just start a song. You establish a deep groove."

I said, "Wow. That's very nice of you to say. I had deep groove teachers: Steve Latanation, Jim Erickson, Rick Thomson, and Brian Fullen!"

Meeting David and the new players was an indication that a New York touring band was being put together. Mary Bailey was removed and replaced by a more powerful manager. I thought it was pretty likely that I would get replaced when the new guy got a look at me.

The unplugged acoustic shows would be over soon. It would have been much easier playing full Shania band shows. But age discrimination is a reality. If you're just an old hired gun, you could be replaced by a younger guitar slinger in a Nashville minute.

Fanfare was coming up. There would be a sea of fans this time. Brian Fullen arranged for a Nashville crew to back Shania at Fan Fair '95. I finally got to play loud and hard with Shania Twain standing next to Brian! The crowd was massive. Fullen counted off the songs. The groove was no longer on my shoulders. The band groove ran deep.

I have one vivid memory of playing with that band: Mutt stood in the photographer section in front of the stage. He listened with his eyes closed. And I promise you—there in the midst of six background singers, drums, bass, guitars, and keyboards, it happened. For one brief second. I played a wrong note. But that's okay, right? There were a dozen other people onstage. At the exact moment that I committed the flub, Mutt opened his eyes and looked right at me. The guy has golden ears. He smiled like a Cheshire cat. I returned a sheepish grin.

Shania's star was skyrocketing. God had given me a front-row seat to see a musical miracle. These things have a season. I was 40 years old. I expected the calls from the newly successful Shania gravy train to stop. They did.

After Fan Fair, I came home to quiet little Franklin, Tennessee. To Lori, Crystal, Randall, and Sarah. They still loved me, even when I didn't have a gig. And Jesus loves me, this I know. Time to get back to songwriting: My kids had grown accustomed to eating. Every day.

Songstory Writer Tip: The song is never finished. There's always something you wish you could change. There are also changes that occur when your song gets recorded. Decades after writing something, your brain still works on it. I guess it's a matter of reaching for perfection. "Why'd You Come In Here Lookin' Like That?" was written as a guy lyric. So, it got changed after it was finished … as if the song wasn't finished. Carrie Underwood recorded it. I bet she changed the melody ever so slightly. I can accept that.

I recently heard Paul Overstreet sing some of his hits. He wrote joke verses to his own songs. It was hilarious. Why would he write more verses after the song became a hit? Because the song is never finished.

Songstory IV

I Picked a Fight with Gilbert Arias

Never started any fights, but I never back down.
I got a clean reputation in this dirty old town.
(Bob Carlisle / Randy Thomas from "Redneck Son"
as recorded by Ty England)

I PICKED A fight with Gilbert Arias. I can't remember why. Right there in junior high art class in 1968. I had been picked on by some really big kids all year. Kids whose only enjoyment seemed to come from drawing blood from younger kids half their size. Junior high was all shoving matches and intimidation, occasionally interrupted by classes. Maybe I had been shoved one too many times.

Gilbert said something. Or maybe he laughed at me. Whatever it was, I got mad. Mad enough to take leave of my senses. So I picked a fight with Gilbert Arias. I looked at him all Clint Eastwood snake-eyed. "Meet me after school." I had called him out. "After school" was like "Noon. OK Corral."

I expected Gilbert to simply apologize. That's what I would have done. No. Gilbert was unflinching when he said, "OK." He seemed to be looking forward to it. That worried me.

The problem with feeling seething anger at 9 A.M. is that all the murderous bravado turns to silent dread by lunchtime. By 2:45 I got scared. Why did I pick a fight with Gilbert Arias? We were both fourteen. He was about my size. But I was all elbows and knobby knees. Gilbert actually had muscles.

Why didn't he just back down? Did he know how to fight? I didn't. I didn't know the first thing about sandlot brawling. I was about to learn. My best junior high buddy was David Lipes. He knew something about fighting because everyone called him David Lips. He said, "Whatever you do, Randy, don't duck out of a fight. You gotta show up." I thought of just sneaking home, where no one ever beat me up. David repeated, "You gotta show." Why did I get myself into this?

So David Lipes and I showed up after school. We were greeted by about seventeen Mexican kids of various sizes. Well, we weren't greeted ... a small army backing up their champion sized us up. Two little gringos with dorky hair and science books. It occurred to me that it might be a bad thing if I won this fight. It might be a *very* bad thing for David Lipes.

The battleground was chosen. The last empty lot in Rialto—off Eucalyptus, north of Frisbee Junior High School—hallowed ground where the nose-blood of teenagers cries out from the ground.

Gilbert seemed to have a plan. I didn't. Gilbert had factored in the fact that I had a mouth full of metal braces. I hadn't. School books were left in the dirt. Mexican kids lined up on one side of the lot. David Lipes stood alone, behind me. The fight began.

The fight started to seem like a knucklehead idea when the knuckles started coming at *my* head. When Gilbert whacked me a few times in the face, I tried to return fire. Then he worked the mouth. Every blow to my mouth mashed my cheeks into the sharp metal on my teeth. The inside of my mouth began to turn to freshly ground beef. The blood tasted like copper.

If my strategy was to wear Gilbert's fists down with my face, it worked. He switched to body blows. I never thought I would welcome a bloodless beating of the ribs. Then came a well-placed punch to the gut. It nearly lifted me off the ground. My lungs seized up. I couldn't breathe.

Something in me appealed to the goodness in human nature. I held up a hand and croaked, "Wait." I was shown mercy. Gilbert could have used that opportunity to finish me off. He didn't. His friends could have turned on the valiant David Lipes. Thank God they didn't. The whole crew of Mexican guys followed their victor home, patting him on the back. I bet none of them ever picked a fight with Gilbert Arias.

David and I walked a couple of miles to his house. On the way, the swelling developed around my eyes and I had to swallow a lot of blood. By the time we put ice on my face, it was too late. One eye was swollen shut. The wires in my mouth were all bent. My orthodontist was going to be apoplectic.

The next day at school, I imagined it would be the end of life for Randy "Fight-Picker" Thomas. I was wrong. Big kids would ask me, "Did you fight Gilbert Arias?"

I would look at the floor and mutter, "Yeah." My right eye was turning beautiful shades of red and blue. Apparently, Gilbert was left-handed.

The big kids said, "Cool."

With the benefit of seventeen hours passing, most of my injuries were hidden inside my mouth and under my shirt. I sat next to Gilbert in art class. A kid asked us, "Did you guys fight yesterday?"

Gilbert nodded and said, "Look at his eye." No one laughed.

Gilbert Arias and I attended art class together without further incident. We were friends after that. The fact that he hadn't killed me when he had the chance made me like him.

The shepherd boy David volunteered to fight Goliath. He was outmatched and looked puny to his opponent, but he fought with God as his strength. I've generally faced mundane obstacles in my life. Still, I desperately need someone in my corner. Someone who sticks closer than a brother. In the coming years, God would prove to me that He had my back. If God is for us, who can be against us? So this was a lesson to prepare me for future lessons.

David Lipes was right. You gotta show up.

Songstory Writer Tip: You've heard this one before. Rule #1 is "show up." How does that work with songwriting? There are times you don't feel like writing. Write something anyway. There are times you won't feel like keeping an appointment with another writer. Keep it anyway.

There is a story that Sinatra once came to the studio where the orchestra was rehearsed and ready to record. Sinatra walked in, looked around, and called out, "Not today, baby!" He left, and all the musicians went home paid. This is a cute story, but a reverse barometer for success.

Most hit songs are the result of someone who was standing around when a song was needed. Maybe he played bass, or had a melody in his head, or suggested a lyric. Whatever the particulars, great songs come from someone being Present. Get it?

No hit song was ever written by the person who wasn't there.

Songstory V

There Must Be a God!

*There is rejoicing in the presence of the angels of God
over one sinner who repents.*
(Luke 15:10)

Thee sounds holier than you, but not holier than Thou.
(Songstory)

I HAD A very early childhood. Sunday mornings meant dressing up in a dark blue blazer and slicking my hair down with Brylcreem. That way, the hair matched the jacket. When we dressed-up kids ran in the sanctuary hallways, a mean old lady shushed us. "This is God's house!" That was my church first lesson. God needs things quiet. Maybe He was sleeping upstairs.

Sunday services are punishment for running free six days a week. I was held hostage between my mother and father. Everyone in church seemed to be 197 years old. The men all had hair coming out of their ears. (I've never forgotten this. Therefore, I tweeze.) There was organ music and everyone was very somber. There was a lot of velvet. I must have gone to a funeral as a kid, because I thought that church meant they were having a funeral. A funeral for Jesus. Shhhh.

In the eulogy, they said nice things about the dearly departed. Jesus fed people. He said, "My peas I leave with you. My peas I give you." They had a picture of Him with folded hands, gazing up into heaven. He was tan and looked like Alan Ladd with long golden hair. I thought, *What if Jesus is messing with us—like Tom Sawyer? Maybe He's hiding in the balcony attending His own funeral service?* Nope. Not in the balcony. Oh, no. What if He's lying dead in that long wooden box that reads, "This Do In Remembrance Of Me"?

Jesus spoke only King James English: "Verily, have ye not read what David didst, when he was an hungred, and did eat the shewbread?" They handed out broken saltine crackers and tiny cups of Welch's grape juice. Even as a kid I thought, *"Jesus deserves a better caterer."*

Once we moved to arid southern California, Sunday became a fun day. No more funerals for Jesus. My dad said it had to do with avoiding something called obligation. I wasn't sure what the word meant. It was something my dad didn't want to feel anymore. I was free to read Doonesbury comic strips and try to figure out what they meant.

It was as if God still had a part-time publicist in the '60s. He had His name in the Pledge of Allegiance. He had honorable mention in a couple of songs. Ethyl Merman used to yell at him real loud to bless America. I'm pretty sure God could hear it. "My Country 'Tis of Thee" was another one. He liked to be called Thee. Thee sounds holier than you, but not holier than Thou. The word "amen" had double meaning. If you said, "AAAYYY-men," it meant you were a Baptist deacon.

The shorter, quieter "a-*men*" meant it was time to eat Thanksgiving turkey.

I think God prefers "AH-men" to "Ay-men." It just sounds smarter.

After childhood, I was never in church, so I guess God had to come looking for *me*. At the age of fourteen, I was on a long walk to see my junior high girlfriend, Lynn. It was a particularly beautiful afternoon. Something changed. Grace came down. It was like the scene in *The Wizard of Oz* where the grainy black-and-white world switches to Technicolor. I was gazing at the mountains in the distance. They gave the impression of being sprinkled with powdered sugar. Giant popcorn clouds dotted the azure sky. A warm breeze blew from the south.

Psalm 19:1 says, "The heavens declare the glory of God; the skies proclaim the work of his hands." Theologians call this "general revelation." I knew nothing of this at the time. I didn't know that the book of Romans begins with God's existence being evidenced by His creation. I only knew my teenage experience at that moment. My heart was surprised by joy. Suddenly, as if I was the first human to think of it, I thought, *There must be a God!* Who made this wonderful world?

I arrived at Lynn's house with a heart overflowing with newfound wonder.

"You know what? I think there must be a God!"

Lynn was taken aback. She squinted. "Well, of course there's a God."

I had no idea that she knew the joy of the clouds and the mountains. "Wow! You think there's a God, too?"

She was confused by my enthusiasm. "Of course. God is the Father, and like the Son, and, uh, the Holy Ghost..."

That was the weirdest thing I'd ever heard. "What? You're saying God has three heads?"

Her face reddened with exasperation. "No. Jesus, Joseph, and Mary!"

Now I was really confused. "Wait. Which one's a ghost?"

Yea, verily, that ended the conversation.

I don't know what happened on that walk in suburbia. I didn't know how to follow up on it. But a switch in my soul had been flipped. It might have been what the Bible terms "regeneration." Titus 3:5 says, "He saved us, not because of works done by us in righteousness, but according to his own mercy, by the washing of regeneration and renewal of the Holy Spirit." Whatever happened that day, the joy lay dormant for over a year.

The seeds of change were sown in the summer of '71. Literally. Our band had pitched in to buy weed. (I know. Stupid is as stupid does.) My buddy Steve had collected the money. The drug dealer was—of course—a pastor's kid. The deal went south when the preacher's kid began preaching about the White Throne Judgment as if he were possessed. He refused to sell the Devil's product. Steve was shaken. He was shaken into becoming a Christian.

We were packing up drums after a rehearsal, and Steve said, "Here's your money back."

"Okay. Why?"

"Well, I just couldn't do it. The preacher's kid told me about Jesus. And I asked Jesus into my life." By some miracle of grace, I immediately knew that this meant that Jesus wasn't lying in the "This Do In Remembrance of Me" box. He was alive!

"Can I?" I asked.

"Can you what?"

"Can I ask Jesus into my life?"

"I guess."

"Any trick to it?"

"Uh, you just try to tell Him all your sins."

"Is that it?"

"Yeah, I think so."

Starting that Monday night, I went home and asked Jesus into my life. I remembered something in the Bible about going into your prayer closet. My closet was too tiny, and the shoes smelled like maybe they needed a funeral. Hm. My grandmother had prayed every night by her bedside. Perhaps that will work. I knelt. I prayed. I named sins. "Jesus, come into my life."

Nothing happened.

Perhaps my expectations were too high. The skies didn't part. No earthquakes. No light from heaven. I kept it up for three days.

Steve invited me to a Wednesday night meeting at the home of Baptist deacon Gillett Doggett. (A name so oddly specific that it must be real.) Steve was there along with a handful of Jesus Freaks, singing songs and listening to Bible stories. They asked me if I had ever asked Jesus into my life. "Yes! I've been trying for three days now!"

A scrawny bearded guy named David Fletcher (may God bless him even now) held out his Bible and showed me John 1:12: "But to all who did receive him, who believed in his name, he gave the right to become children of God." Dave explained that religious or emotional experiences may come and go, but the promises of God were permanent. It was the shortest Bible lesson of my life. One that I never forgot.

There were many emotional experiences to come later. And much confusion. After all, we were young Jesus Freaks reading 1611 King James English about a Jewish culture in Roman-occupied Israel! Verily, I saith unto thee, it confoundeth the soul.

Steve, Gillett and David got me off on a sure footing. My relationship with God is based on His promises and not my experiences. On that third day He was risen. I walked home under the stars that night in Rialto, saying to myself, "I'm a Christian now. I'm a Christian."

From that summer on, a Parrish blue sky continued to glow in Technicolor over my black and white everyday world.

Songstory Writer Tip: How do you write Christian songs? If you are a Christian, and you write a song, I might argue that you have written a Christian song. Christians experience doubt, loneliness, and fear. Not all your songs need to preach. Actually, the preachier you get, the lesslier it will work.* Here's what will always work: Use scripture.

What is very rare is a Christian song that tells a story. This is ironic, since the Bible tells a story. Two of my story-song examples are "Valerie" and "Juliana Wilson." A greater example would be Don Francisco's songs from the early '80s. He told Bible stories. Sweet Comfort Band once toured with Don. He was supposed to open for us. The problem was, his songs were so impactful that they got a standing ovation. Starting with the second date, the band told Don, "We'll open for you."

One guy with an acoustic guitar and Bible stories. It's one of the most powerful things I've ever seen. Look up "He's Alive." It tells the story of the resurrection from Peter's perspective. It's astounding. Dolly Parton even performed it on her *White Limozeen* record along with "Why'd You Come In Here Lookin' Like That?" It's the last song on the record. It's so strong, no other song wants to follow it.

---

* "The preachier you get, the lesslier it will work." This is both a quirky quotable quote and an example of a songwriter making up words when it suits the narrative. Which is fun. Like Mairzy Doats and Dozy Doats. Drives spell-check crazy! People say "You can't make this stuff up!" I say you can.

Songstory VI

Bad Day at Black Rock (Learning How Songs Compose Your Life)

Anything worth doing is worth doing badly.
(G.K. Chesterton)

RIALTO, CALIFORNIA, IN the 1960s was a suburban paradise right out of *The Truman Show*. Add in kids on skateboards wearing surfer cross necklaces. The Hollies playing on the radio. The smell of freshly mowed lawns filled the air. Palm tree–lined boulevards. Historic Route 66 bustled two blocks away. American culture was flexing its muscles as the world watched in admiration.

My grade school teachers labeled me the Absent-Minded Professor. I was the dorky kid staring out the window, daydreaming. In spite of this, I got top marks.

My dad was the high school band director. He was a true consumer of music. All the eras and styles of music were played in our home. Growing up in a constant music appreciation class was probably the key in the development of my song awareness.

Sixties rock and pop was the starting line for me as a future songwriter. My older brother and sister were listening to the current records of the day. It was my brother Larry who announced to me, "I've written a song."

I was intrigued. "You have? Let's hear it!"

My brother sang me something that sounded like Jan and Dean meet the Beach Boys. It was good enough that it stuck in my mind.

By the next day I had turned that (long lost) melody and lyric around in my head. I could hear what the drums, guitars, and bass should play. My young brain worked out Beach Boys–style harmonies, complete with soaring Brian Wilson parts singing "Oooweeeoo" on top, undergirded with Papa-oomowmow-type bass parts.

The next day, I sang all the parts for my brother. I think he was shocked. "Hey, that's really good!" he said. High praise from an eighteen-year-old to a ten-year-old. The song was forgotten, but not the "I can do this" feeling!

Years later, my next lesson was about collaboration. My best friend Steve showed me a lyric about a guy robbing a liquor store with a fake gun. I put chords to his melody. Within a few minutes, we had written a song called "Bad Day at Black Rock." I still remember Steve's lyrics:

What a day, I gotta say, I feel I'm getting very bored.
I know what I can do, I'm gonna rob a liquor store!
I'm carving a gun from an old piece of wood;
dip it in black paint- it looks pretty good...
Bad Day at Black Rock, baby. Bad day today....

It was terrible. But it was fun!

The songwriting muse was stalking me, but I was too unaware to notice. Our garage band, Sunrise, covered the rock and pop songs of the early 1970s. This taught me two things: how to re-create rock songs on guitar, and how those songs were structured. I think it's fair to say that if you can learn to play an instrument, you can learn to write songs. (Getting to be really great at either of those takes some doing…) Song crafting can be learned. I think my rate of improvement was quite slow, but the ground you gain is never lost.

My first few attempts were some of the worst songs in the history of bad songs. In 1972 I became a Christian. Is this when my songs rose to a higher level? NO! Probably thanks to the forbearing nature of Christian audiences—it got worse! When I began writing preachy songs that rhymed "died for me on Calvary," our audiences were probably too forgiving. Ah, but we were juveniles. And most creatures are cute when they are young.

We were teaching ourselves how to master our instruments. The dance band Sunrise became the Christian band Sonrise. We started kicking around original songs. My early efforts may not have been good, but at least they were longer than *Lord of the Rings*. A concert was held in 1974 at Pacific High School. On the same bill were Sonrise, Psalm 150, and Sweet Comfort. I would wind up playing in all three of those bands.

Psalm 150 was an Orange County, California, "horn" band, with Greg Eckler as the undisputed leader. Jack Blades was on bass in those days. Jack went on to form Night Ranger and Damn Yankees. I joined Psalm 150 after Andraé Crouch borrowed some band members and never gave them back. Sam Scott and I traveled with Psalm 150 until Bob Carlisle and Greckler formed a yacht club band. On that day, Psalm 150 was over.

The Riverside trio Sweet Comfort had an unusual advantage: They had a singer, Bryan Duncan, who wrote his own songs! By 1976, I had been grafted into that band.

If you listen to the *Sweet Comfort* album, I think you might agree that my debut song, "His Name Is Whispered," is not the pick of the litter! Producer Tommy Coomes had this idea that songs should be re-arranged. He took my typical arrangement and made it into an odd verse, chorus, bridge (surprise), verse, chorus affair. We thought it was brilliant at the time. In retrospect, it was just shuffling the cards on a mediocre hand.

Bryan wrote most of the strong material on that record. While rehearsing to record, Bryan started playing around with "When I Was Alone" and jacked it up to the tempo of "Crocodile Rock." I wrote a second section on the spot. ("Oh, let me lay it down.") In a matter of minutes, we had a new song entitled "Childish Things."

It's the same music on two songs. Just a change in tempo and my little chorus. To top it off, this happy pop tune was played nationwide! In neighboring San Bernardino, California, we had a pop station called KFXM (Tiger Radio). Imagine our glee when "Childish Things" went to number 11 on our local rock station. What an amazing joy it is to hear your song being broadcast in your home town, blasting from your own car!

(Later, we learned that having a top-twenty hit on one station means bupkus in the music business. You have to be on stations in every market to have a real hit.)

Prior to the *Sweet Comfort* record, I had a song in my back pocket. My buddy Sam Scott had written a praise song. At that time, praise songs were a new thing. I began leading worship at Calvary Chapel in Riverside (now Harvest Christian Fellowship). Greg Laurie was our 23-year-old pastor.

Pastor Bob Probert would often do music prior to Saturday night concerts. It was very casual. No one knew that worship leading would later become a thing. Bob or Greg might ask me to lead songs—alone, armed only with an acoustic guitar. We often sang very simple choruses. There were no lyrics, screens, or charts in those days. I noticed that some of my favorite Calvary Chapel choruses had a counterpoint part for the girls.

I had the idea to simplify Sam's song and write a girls' part for it. ("Birds in the sky sing their song to you...") Then I wanted to see how it worked with the large Calvary Chapel crowd. It *worked*. Hearing a thousand voices singing something you made up in your head is quite a thing. The new song must have caused a buzz.

Bob Probert called. "They're recording your song for a Maranatha praise album."

I said, "What? It's Sam's song. I just wrote a girls' part to it!"

I drove out to Costa Mesa to Whitefield studio, which was the home of many early Maranatha records. Guess who was producing? Tommy Coomes! He had heard me sing the song at Calvary Riverside. I watched the production as an outsider. The *Praise 3* album came out and "I Want to Praise You, Lord" became an international hit! There have been multiple spin-off recordings.

Of course, the business side of music is always where it gets weird. My publisher was Lexicon. The head of publishing said, "You should sign the publishing over to us," so like a dolt, I did. Sam and I split the songwriting credit. If I had it to do over again (man, that's a phrase you hear a lot in business), Sam and I would have retained *all* the publishing rights. We signed away fifty percent of the pie to a little company that had nothing to do with getting the song cut! This was the common deal.

Oh, well. You have to look at plus side: Sam and I were paid a bit in royalties every year. But, unlike a disposable pop song, "I Want to Praise You, Lord" lived a long life. It was sung for decades. It is still sung in many languages across the globe.

Soon after, I wrote "We Must Wait on the Lord." That was another major Maranatha praise song. This time around, I showed up for the recording session. Smart move. I got to play on the basic track with Kelly Willard (piano) and many other fine musicians. This enabled me to influence the key, tempo, and arrangement of the song. I love how it turned out.

Many of the original Maranatha band members used to do background vocals on the Praise series recordings. Michele Pillar was with us on one of those sessions. It was around 1977. We were in a group of eight or ten singers. Producer Tommy Coomes said, "Someone is a little flat."

I sang the part terribly and joked, "It's YOU, Michele! You're *flat!*"

She swiftly retorted, "Yes. But I've got great legs!"

Songstory Writer Tip: A pro writer knows that his or her song will be changed. You record your demo to be just that: a demonstration of the song. It documents it. The key, tempo, lyrics, and arrangement are subject to an artist's needs. Sometimes they are subject to an artist's whims. I know of a female country star who recorded the National Anthem incorrectly. When asked to re-record her vocal, she resisted, saying, "Can't you just get the writer to change it?"

I remember when Bob Carlisle and I were listening to Hank Williams Jr. singing our song "I'm Tired." He didn't get our original phrasing. He didn't get it at all. Hank made up his own.

I don't know about you, but I'm not going to argue with Hank Williams Jr. He seems that he might fight dirty.

Songstory VII

Ash Trays, Hell, and Wine

The cemeteries are full of indispensable men.
—Original source uncertain (presumed dead)

MY FIRST DAY job was selling circus tickets by phone. "Hello! This is Randy Thomas with the San Bernardino County Sheriff's Department. How are you today?" People get downright rattled when they think a sheriff is calling. After the First Pitch, some callees figured out that I might be a college student working a dead-end night job. If they said, "No, thank you," then I would read the Second Pitch: "That's fine if you don't want to enjoy the circus this year! Perhaps you'd prefer to buy some tickets for underprivileged children at the School of Hope?" Then the poor unwilling customer would be forced to say something like, "No, thank you. I don't want to sponsor children. I'm a heartless miser."

There was a lot of manipulation in sales. There were a lot of ash trays, too. The top salesman in my office was a guy who faked a posh English accent and smoked a pack of cigarettes per shift. I lasted only a few weeks. Given the choice between a career in cold calls ending with cancer, or the unknown—I took the unknown.

Some of us in Sonrise got jobs at Beverly Manor in San Bernardino. It was a "psychiatric facility" in 1974.

That means the guests were there on an involuntary basis. I was an orderly whose extensive nursing training took all of twenty minutes. (I had to make a bed like a Marine recruit. A skill that I have conveniently forgotten.)

My lack of nursing knowledge was offset by large female nurses who knew how to throw their weight around. When there was an "episode," a Nurse Brock would hold down a patient while shooting him up with thorazine. My assignment was to restrain the resident with a straight jacket and wrist contraptions that are probably illegal today. Most of the job required cleaning up stuff that came out of people. All the Beverly Manor robes read, "B.M." I bet I know why.

I learned new anatomical terms at Beverly Manor. There was a lady who tripped the alarm while trying to leave the building naked. (Not that the building was naked. The patient was.) I said, "Mildred, you can't go outside like that!"

She said, "Like what?"

I pointed at her chest. "Like that."

Mildred looked down and then waved me off. "Oh, those are just my McDuffys!"

On my first week, I encountered the diminutive Uldine Utley. Converted by the famous Aimee Semple McPherson in 1921, Uldine became a famed Pentecostal child evangelist. By the age of fourteen, she was preaching at Madison Square Garden. By 1938, she was committed to a sanitarium. I knew none of this when I met her. I remember our first conversation:

"Good morning Uldine!" (I pronounced it Ul-dine.)

She glowered at me, pointed a boney finger up at my nose, and cackled, "It's Yool-DEEN! I'm walking through a field of clover that you just *murdered!* And when I get out, I'm going to send you to the Third Level of HELL!" The word "hell" echoed down the white hallways, while soothing music drifted out of hidden ceiling speakers.

Now you see why I remember her so well.

It didn't take a degree in psychology to deduce that Uldine had developed three distinct personalities. Her evil preacher personality made pronouncements like, "I baptize you in the name of the Father, and of the Son, and of the Holy Ghost—D@MN YOU!" Then there was a petrified Uldine who was convinced that They were coming after her:

"They're coming for me! Hide me!"

"Who are 'they,' Uldine?"

"The Beast and the Prophet! I've told them. I don't believe in Jesus! I don't! I DON'T!"

One day a chatty, angelic Uldine followed me on my rounds, telling me about her neighbors. She loved everyone. She pronounced her name UL-dine, which I think is the proper enunciation. This is the little girl with an Oklahoma accent that I'd like to think was the original Uldine. She was the sweetest sixty-year-old child you'd ever want to meet.

There were many other Beverly Manor episodes that are burned into my memory. I'll let Mildred and Uldine serve as representatives. I loved all my Beverly Manor people, but they were much better off with orderlies who knew what they were doing. And that excluded me.

Next, I worked for Campus Crusade for Christ. That sounds more fitting, right? Except that they expected me to cut my hair and wear a tie. I cut my hair. We signed documents that stated we would not smoke, drink, or cuss while at work. Many of the employees were Baptists who would never be caught drinking. (Oh, they might drink, but they would never be *caught*.)

Some warehouse workers would argue all day. One argument was that Jesus never drank wine. I asked one co-worker, "Are you sure? Why the miracle at Cana? And you think Jesus and the disciples had Welch's at Passover?"

He clenched his jaw. "Well, I'll tell you this: Jesus didn't drink wine. And if He *did*, I wouldn't have anything to do with Him!"

We packed and shipped boxes all day long. Still to this day, when I see a cardboard box, I remember the dusty warehouse full of brown boxes, brown tape, brown desks, brown coffee, brown floors, brown walls, and brown air.

When the brown warehouse work slowed, they sent me to work "up on the hill." After a gorgeous drive up the mountain, I'd work all day at Campus Crusade headquarters in the stately Arrowhead Springs Hotel. What a gorgeous setting! (Mental music cue: "The Sound of Music.") Built in 1905, this became the party place for the Hollywood stars in later decades. We're talking Judy Garland, the Marx brothers, and Bogart and Bacall.

Behind the hotel was an arrowhead-shaped swimming pool, mirroring the huge shape on the face of the mountain. This is a "natural" (unexplainable) 1,400-foot arrowhead formed of white sagebrush. Indians say the Great Spirit burned the head of his arrow into the hillside, pointing down to the healing hot springs.

By 1975, the breathtaking hotel was a bit run down. Crusade didn't have the funds to update such a grand estate. Some of the rugs and drapes dated back to the 1940s. What had been opulent was now threadbare.

I would often see Dr. Bill Bright in the hallways. Of course, I was just the young guy with disco hair vacuuming the worn carpet. Bill Bright had gone from being a candy salesman to a very practical evangelist. He was the Walt Disney of Evangelicalism to me. It was an honor to clean toilets and set tables for Campus Crusade visitors from around the world.

Our band guys would drive up to the hotel late at night. The natural hot springs were inside the mountain, deep under the old hotel. No one ever ventured into those old tunnels at night, except us Jesus Freaks. We would soak in the hot mineral waters. In those days, I guess the old caves there were all but forgotten. We had it to ourselves. I pictured Tony Curtis and Marilyn Monroe hanging out there in the '50s.

We also thought it was odd that people would buy Arrowhead Springs "100% mountain spring water." The natural springs in the cave smelled like sulfur! I mean, who would ever buy bottled water? That makes as much sense as listing your chapters in Roman numerals: It'll never catch on.*

When business picked up at the warehouse, they brought me back to the brown hell. I mean, warehouse.

Crusade had an annoying habit of sending us a green-behind-the-ears supervisor every few months. It would be a college grad who had textbook ideas of how to rule a brown kingdom. This way, the only person who knew nothing about the warehouse was in charge.

I graduated to "truck wrapper." This didn't mean I wrapped trucks. It meant putting together pallets of books to load onto trucks. I remember the sweltering summer of 1976. Our supervisor told my Lutheran buddy and me to off-load a truck. He directed the truck driver to back up INTO the warehouse. This had never been done before. Two of us unloaded what seemed like a ton of books out of the big trailer. We were getting time-and-a-half pay for staying past 5 o'clock. ($3.00 an hour!) The driver was in such a hurry that he helped us. We worked up a serious sweat. The supervisor signed the paperwork and told the driver he could leave.

With the advantage of hindsight, I can understand how unloading so many boxes would cause that trailer to rise. And rise it did. It must have gone up into the ceiling. So, when the truck pulled out, parts of warehouse ceiling pulled out, too. I saw the driver looking in his mirrors. He was probably late to pick up another load (or possibly

---

* Why Roman numerals? Why not Arabic? So I could tell this joke: A Roman walks into a coffee shop. Says, "Five coffees, please." Holds up two fingers...

he didn't want an insurance hassle), so he gunned it, taking parts of the warehouse with him. As the ceiling cracked open, the sprinkler system above us burst forth like a spring shower!

It's hard to describe how funny the scene was: the new supervisor staring open-mouthed up at the ravaged warehouse ceiling while my sweaty co-worker and I danced in the rain!

And that was my career in day jobs. The feckless supervisor who replaced the former supervisor had an issue with my absences with Sweet Comfort Band. He told me I would have to choose between committing to the brown Crusade warehouse job or traveling around the country playing music with a Christian rock band.

It wasn't a difficult decision to make.

Songstory Writer Tip: The final touch on a song is the arrangement. This is where writers often fall short. Sometimes record producers re-arrange your song. Why not make it great from the start? Try writing an intro that is not the verse or chorus music. Listen to "Does Anybody Really Know What Time It Is?" I know it's an elaborate example, but I've seen an arena cheering the introduction. That's what you want.

Check out arrangements on hit songs. You might hear a double first verse. Some songs (like Def Leppard) have a singalong chorus followed by another chorus. Brilliant! A majority of hits have a bridge. A popular trick is the double chorus at the end. In some cases, repeating your opening line makes a great ending.

Learn about writing what we call B-sections, or ramps. This is the add-on to your verse that takes you to the chorus. A worship song trick is to write a bridge that you can sing over the chorus. ("How Great Is Our God.") And the oldest trick in the book is the tag. You can repeat the last two lines of your chorus before ending.

I work with the assumption that every song needs to have all these options (and more) thrown at it, to see which ones improve it. Sound like too much work? Just imagine twenty thousand people singing along...

Songstory VIII

The Jesus Movement

Without music to decorate it, time is just a bunch
of boring production deadlines
or dates by which bills must be paid.
(Frank Zappa)

Here's the thing, kids.
There actually was a world before you got here.
(Bill Maher)

WE NOW LIVE in a church that has forgotten the Jesus Movement. For those of us who were involved, it was a counter to the counter-culture movement. It was like antidisestablishmentarianism. (Not the longest word in the dictionary, but it will do.) The Jesus Movement picked up where the hippies left off. Early Jesus Freaks were refugees from a Hippie Dream that became a nightmare.

I first saw hippies in San Francisco in the late '60s. They were scary. The ones I saw were unkempt panhandlers and druggies. I was a cowardly suburban long-hair who showered regularly. If loving Grateful Dead music is the dividing line, then a hippie I am not. Hendrix and Cream—the frilly paisley freaks—were more my style.

David Fletcher would drive us out to Calvary Chapel Costa Mesa on a Saturday night. Dave's rickety Chevy Corvair often smelled strongly of gas fumes. Jesus Freaks try to avoid hallucinogenics, so we trundled along in the California night air with the windows down.

We would arrive at a large tent. The hippie girls all wore granny dresses. The guys generally had full beards and long hair in an attempt to look like Jesus. Most freaks carried a thick King James Bible. Sandals were the common footwear (adding to the Jesus vibe). The Father-Son-Holy Ghost language was not spoken here. The most common term was "the Lord." Everyone talked about the Lord. Everyone praised the Lord!

I heard stories of a Lonnie Frisbee. He had an appearance that nailed the '60s image of Jesus. Lonnie was a leader in the Jesus Movement before I became aware of it. Because of his struggle with homosexuality and his later involvement in the Vineyard movement, Lonnie became He Who Shall Not Be Named. It was only privately that I heard about Lonnie's influence. He was sort of erased.

Tom Stipe was the first Calvary Chapel preacher who I met. Tom didn't meet the typical hippie profile. He was a smiling chubby guy with a magnetic sense of humor. I would put Stipey up against any comedian of the day. When he preached on the plagues of Egypt, they came alive with humor. The plague of frogs, for example:

So frogs come up over the land. They're everywhere. Look in the oven—"Ribbit!" [Laughter.] Look in the breadbox—"Ribbit!" [Laughter.] Pull down the sheets on the bed—"Ribbit!" [Laughter.] So Pharaoh's magicians see this and they work their magic; POOF! And, oh hey, this is

great—they drum up a few MORE FROGS! That's
a big help … thanks, guys! "Ribbit!" [Laughter]

Before a preacher spoke, there would be music. The
music was so great. (Bear in mind that I was seventeen
years old, and the musicians were in their impressive
early twenties.) It could be Children of the Day, Karen
Lafferty, LoveSong, The Way, or a few other home-grown
Jesus bands. I'm not sure if it the music was so incredible,
or if it was the prayer-soaked Holy Spirit atmosphere, or
both. The concerts were enthralling. They always ended
with the altar call. Bow your eyes and close your head.

There was a Jesus People humor, too. Oden Fong
was with Mustard Seed Faith. His father, Benson Fong,
had played in Charlie Chan movies and many TV shows
including *My Three Sons*. I was nervous meeting him.

Oden was sitting on a bench with his leg in a cast. I
asked, "What happened to your leg?"

Oden answered, "The Holy Ghost fell on me." That's
heavy, man.

I dragged all my friends to Calvary Costa Mesa.
And sometimes they took me. It was such a revelation
to see new, cool music being sung for Jesus! There was
a personal revelation in it for us. Michael, Steve, and I
realized *We can do this, too!* We weren't as good as these
musicians—yet.

As Sonrise, we began playing at my local church. I
can see and quote the sign out on the north lawn: "Rialto
Community Baptist Church, Raeburn E. Woodson,
Pastor." A youth pastor let us play during a Wednesday

night event. I think it was jarring to have a whole band of long-hairs play in that little church. There was a definite tension between what we were trying to do and what churches would accept. Rialto was not as cutting-edge as Costa Mesa.

Since a prophet is not without honor, except in Rialto, we looked to nearby San Bernardino. Michael found an Assembly of God church. We're talking beehive hairdos. The women had them, too. The church was innocuously renamed San Bernardino Community Church. The older people yearned for the olden days when aisles were for dancing in the Spirit, and the altar was where you were slain in the Spirit. Glory.

It was in this church that I must admit I heard the most confusing sermons of my life. The idea of planning a sermon was contrary to the mysterious working of the Holy Spirit, so the sermon rambled, or rumbled, or screamed, or cried without much rhyme or reason. BUT—they let us play there on Saturday nights!

This became our home for years, while we learned to play as a band. Pastor Vince Neypes masterfully manned the church piano. He would become the mentor to us freaks. The sanctuary was orange, red, and yellow, as if the building were on fire. (That was the intended effect.) The Holy Ghost Dove was artfully depicted in orange and yellows, as if it were going down in flames onto the platform.

Saturday night became what we called a Koinonia concert series. I don't recall ever being paid for playing. We all had day jobs so we could chip in on the offering.

While Costa Mesa had its large crowds of Jesus Freaks, we brought the Jesus Movement to San Bernardino. The church developed a rich community of college-age Jesus people.

We had been swept up in a tidal wave. Of course, it was a spiritual phenomenon, so we were often amazed at how the outside world largely ignored our Jesus subculture. There was great excitement living in the last days. Jesus was coming back. We were ready. We became musical missionaries.

Sam, Bob, and I wound up in the horn band Psalm 150. Only Sarcasm was spoken in that band. We spoke in Opposites. If the drummer was getting on your nerves, you might say, "You're new. And getting newer." It was hilarious for a while. Let's just say it got new.

Where did this collection of musical freaks come from? Let's get back to Rialto in the days before disco...

Songstory Writer Tip: A great song foundation is a "riff." Examples of riff songs abound. When I was a kid, we had "Sunshine of Your Love" and "In-A-Gadda-Da-Vida." On "Man with a Mission," Bob sings with my slide guitar riff. In recent years, "Uptown Funk" starts with and incorporates a riff. A riff can be so strong that in most cases, the lyrics don't really matter much. If you are great at music and struggle with lyrics, look to the mighty riff to bail you out. The above examples happen to be all two-bar riffs. Think of that. You may be two bars away from the next "Louie Louie."

So much music today is simple chords with no great riff. Maybe you could buck that trend. The key to a riff is sing-ability. You're looking for catchy. You're looking for a hook to put more hooks over. The formula has worked a thousand times. It will work again!

Songstory IX

From Rathole to Charles Manson

Sometimes you will never know the value of a moment
until it becomes a memory.
(Dr. Seuss)

IN THE '70S there were two modes of band transportation: Ford vans and Chevy vans. There was an unwinnable argument as to which was better. In the early days we used a 1960s station wagon that had been waxed once. We knew this because the white swirls had never been wiped off and were now permanent.

My ride was a battleship-sized, butter-yellow, 1968 Chrysler Newport Custom. With a massive 440 c.i.d. motor, mileage was measured in gallons per mile. Gas was 33 cents a gallon. Scientists announced that fossil fuel was scheduled to become extinct by 1980. Now, I'm a fossil that remembers those days.

I have so many traveling adventures to get to. I'll sprinkle them throughout *Songstory*. Let's return to those days of flared jeans and runaway inflation!

Dr. Feelgood in Cold Blood

The date was February 14, 1971. Steve Latanation (a fellow band director's son), Jim McGarvey, and I played our first paid date at Rialto Junior High, affectionately known as "Rathole." For lack of a band name, Jim unilaterally decided on Marsh Fields. Jim's mother had made us matching red vests with white letters that read "M.F."

I don't know about your junior high, but M.F. was not interpreted as Marsh Fields in my junior high. Ahem. We didn't wear the M.F. vests.

The length of a dance is always three hours. It's a law. Our scrawny power trio knew about seven songs. There was another four we could fake. Yeah, we ran out of material. Steve recalls that I had an epiphany borne out of necessity. I announced, "And now, by special request, we are going to play 'Proud Mary.' Again. Thank you!" With that excuse, we repeated the song. I kept introducing songs as special requests until our three hours were expended. We were paid $60.

SIXTY DOLLARS.

The fools. I don't think any of us had clutched a twenty-dollar bill before.

Another professional milestone was being booked out of town. Local San Bernardino D.J. Chris Roberts arranged for us to play at Apple Valley Junior High School. It was a two-hour drive to an unknown oasis. Jesus was right: "A prophet is not without honor, except in his own country." Our band was not a big deal at home, but we were stars at Apple Valley Junior High!

After the dance, some of the girls wanted goodbye kisses. We felt like the Beatles. We were paid an astounding $250! Even more astounding was finding out that D.J. Chris had gotten a $250 deposit for booking the band—$250 for a phone call. It was our second lesson in the music business.

We three terminally white kids teamed with five twenty-something black singers from San Bernardino for a club engagement in a bad part of Bakersfield. By this time, we called ourselves Dr. Feelgood. The seasoned singers were known as In Cold Blood. So in Bakersfield, we became "Dr. Feelgood In Cold Blood"! Each night began with our pimply white trio playing Cream and Creedence. They hated us. Perhaps "hate" is too mild a word. Judging by the wine bottles being thrown at our heads, they wanted to kill us! Then the singers would come out and do old R&B. The crowd loved them! The highlight of the show was the stage jokes:

Man:	"Telegram!"
Woman:	"Is it a singing telegram?"
Man:	"No, ma'am. Just a regular telegram..."
Woman:	"Oh, please! Please sing it to me!"
Man:	(Shrugs) "All right." (Sings) *"Your sister Freda's dead and so your mama said you'd better come home right awaaaay..."*

The lead singer was "Saint." He was in charge. He was large. We were holed up in the fleabag motel next to the nightclub. (Actually, the fleas had moved to a nicer motel.) Saint instructed us to run up a tab with the café. The chatty ladies there fed us soul food that was heavenly! At the end of our week, Saint woke us up in the middle of the night. "Pack up. We're leaving." We were three hours from home. We didn't dare ask too many questions and lose our ride.

While some strange substances were being smoked in the car, Saint explained what was going on. "The club was gonna stiff us, man. So, we ran out on the hotel and café bills. Let them work it out." I sure didn't like stiffing those sweet ladies who fed us so well.

Bleary-eyed, I asked, "What about paying us band members?"

Saint gave me a stern you-better-trust-me look. "Don't worry about that. I'll pay you at home. I'll get the money from my ladies." Ladies? Um, did that mean Saint was a pimp? Yep. The other singers assured me that Saint had ladies.

We made it home to San Bernardino. We were out two weeks' work, plus items stolen from our room. The band was never paid. Just as well. I didn't want money taken from "ladies." That was our third lesson in the music business.

Another breakthrough was playing the Aquarius Club in San Bernardino. For teenagers, a nightclub was a big deal. The band was now Sunrise. We had Michael Hodge (now with Lakewood Church in Houston) on guitar, John Smaha on keys, and Joel Madden on bass. Steve and I remained the foundation through membership changes.

Chris Roberts was supplying me with forty-five singles from the KFXM playlist. Our band had a jump on learning top radio hits as they were released. One we didn't use was "Bye Bye Miss American Pie." It had too many verses to memorize!

The Aquarius was our first grownup gig. Mike and I rented amps, so that the tiny stage looked impressive. We lost money playing that week. A lesson in mathematics.

By 1972, the band members had become Christians. Jesus Freaks. It was a shock playing coffee houses and Christian venues. Why so? Volume. We had grown up playing as loudly as we could. Louder is better. So, we had two problems: we had to play quietly as church mice, and we needed songs.

We took songs like "Listen to the Music" and made it into "Listen to the Spirit." Plus, I began to write songs. Bad songs. And by saying "bad," I'm being generous.

Sunrise became Sonrise. Our first gig was at Rialto Community Baptist Church. We opened for a band called Blessed Hope. There was an apocalyptic invitation to receive Christ at the end of the night. Joel came forward! So the joke became "We've found that it really improved our ministry once our bass player got saved!"

Our lives were further changed by meeting Psalm 150 in Highland, California. They were polished players. Watching Jaymes Felix play guitar changed my garage-band thinking. My low-slung guitar came upward. I learned to use my pinky finger.

We played the little communes and churches around southern California. One odd place was the Vine. People danced and prophesied. They had a Psalm 96 tune they would sing non-stop:

Oh, let the heavens rejoice, and let the earth be glad, let the seas roar and the fullness thereof; let the fields be joyful and all that is within before the Lord! For he cometh, he cometh, to judge the earth; he cometh to judge the earth—and he will rule the world with his righteousness and the people with his truth!

I promise you I wrote this from memory! Songwriters/ worship leaders/teachers: There is great power in repetition. It's an incredible learning tool. Now, back to our story.

After I joined Psalm 150, we were sent out by Hotline Christian Fellowship to play in prisons. California must have a prison population the size of Australia. We played nearly every major penitentiary. Equipment was searched going in and coming out.

A hippie chaplain (known as Pastor Fly, since he looked like a fly) told me, "The first rule in prison is— if you're a fake, a snitch, or a hypocrite, you're dead. I became a Christian in the joint. One night, when I came back to my room, someone grabbed me from behind and put a knife to my throat. He said, 'If you're a Jesus Freak, I'm gonna kill you.' I was scared, but I said, 'Go ahead, then; because I'm for real.' Whoever it was threw me against the bed and left. And you know what? Nobody bothered me after that."

Psalm 150 alternated playing churches and prisons. It taught me an unfortunate reality: most church people wouldn't pass the knife-to-the-throat test. They clean up on the outside. By contrast, prisoners present themselves as badder than they are and tend to be honestly broken inside. A broken person is quicker to "get" the Gospel (James 1:22–25).

Psalm 150 played San Quentin, near San Rafael. Charles Manson was imprisoned there. In the 1970s, the infamous Tate/LaBianca serial slayings carried out by the Manson Family had repulsed the nation. Society was shocked at the involvement of three young women. After the cases were tried, it became clear that Tex Watson and the girls had carried out the murders, while Manson was the puppet master that instigated the carnage.

I asked a San Quentin guard, "Will we see Manson?"

He said, "Wanna see Manson, huh?" He took me around a corner and said, "See that maximum security building? Inside that building is another building, and inside that is another, and in the middle of all that is the room where Manson is. This is as close to seeing Manson as anyone's gonna get! If he ever did get out, he'd be dead in two minutes. Everyone in this pen wants to be the guy who killed Charles Manson."

I thanked the guard, and I never asked about Manson again.

In 1975, Psalm 150 played at the California Men's Colony in San Luis Obispo. We did a Saturday night concert for the general population. There were two rules that applied to all inmates: They all smoked, and they were all innocent. Our brand of hard funk and Greg's approach of no-nonsense preaching worked well with these hard cases.

The leader of the Christian inmates at CMC was a quiet guy named Charlie. Charlie looked a bit like Mr. Spock from Star Trek, except that he had a shy grin. I was haggard and tired when we did this particular Saturday night smoke-fest concert for all the "innocent" prisoners.

We came back the next Sunday morning to do a chapel service for the Christians who attended. There was Charlie again. He was so kind that I fell under conviction about being Mr. Grumpy Pants the night before. After the worship service, I sat down with Charlie to apologize. I said, "Man, you were a great example of love and humility last night; please forgive me." He was very gracious.

Then one of the chapel-attending prisoners asked him, "Hey, Tex! Where do we put these chairs?"

I said, "I thought your name was Charlie." Then I looked at his laundry mark on his shirt: *Watson*. "Wait … you're Tex Watson?"

He replied quietly, "Yes, sir."

This was one of the most astounding moments of my life. I had just told a world-famous serial killer that I was convicted by his loving example. This was a humble southerner who had been quietly and miraculously transformed by the grace of God. I had sensed this before I became aware of who he was as a criminal.

Many people are uncomfortable with the idea that a murderer can be forgiven. His victims are still dead.

Watson's actions caused an enormous amount of pain. Charlie is the only inmate I met who looked me in the eye and said, "I did it. I'm guilty." He talked of Manson's diabolical ability to influence and control his hippie family. Charlie said, "I thought he was Jesus." After being imprisoned, Tex began to listen to a prison chaplain and read Christian materials sent to him by his mother. God's Word and prayer led to his conversion.

If you don't believe it's possible for someone like Charlie to become a true believer, then I suggest that you don't understand the full power of the Gospel. Jesus died for sinners (Romans 5:8). His sacrifice covers the most heinous sins, including murder. The crimes he committed and the losses are still there; Charlie deserves the death sentence. So do I. We are not forgiven because we say "I'm sorry." We are forgiven because God the Father laid on Jesus the crimes that Charlie and I should hang for. Jesus hung in our stead. That is the Gospel.

By the way, Charlie spent the afternoon with us and walked freely all around the prison. He accompanied us to the last security check. All the guards and inmates knew him and seemed to respect him. What a contrast to how Manson was hidden away. We said goodbye to this redeemed murderer who is our brother.

Songstory Writer Tip: Repetition is a major power tool in your bag of tricks. I remember every word of the theme song from *Gilligan's Island*. I don't think I heard it that many times, but it has stayed in my memory banks for fifty-plus years. I memorized part of John 14 as well. Still have it, fifty years later.

There are multiple ways to use repetition. You can have musical phrases that repeat a rhythm while varying the notes. A song's chorus is the primary vehicle that may get replayed four times. If a second verse repeats the melody of the first verse, it introduces new lyrics, right?

Be careful not to overdo repetition (unless you are writing a ten-second jingle or a bad worship song). Also, be careful not to overdo repetition. (See?)

Use subtle changes to mask your repetition. (Notice how reading the word "repetition" four times in quick succession causes irritation!) The end of "Hey Jude" would drive me crazy (or even more crazy) were it not for the lead vocal screaming over it. Try changing up your chorus lyric to mask the potential for listener burnout.

"Butterfly Kisses" follows the standard V/C/V/C/ Bridge/C format. Take note: the chorus lyrics *changed*. Hit songs are usually a mix of elements of predictability with the element of surprise.

There. I've given you the keys to the songwriter kingdom. Now, what are you going to do with them?

Songstory X

Slim and None

Nothing in this world can take the place of persistence.
Talent will not: nothing is more common than
unsuccessful men with talent.
(Calvin Coolidge)

I NEVER INTENDED to join Sweet Comfort Band. Perhaps it was like a Monkees thing. They needed a Peter Tork. Sweet Comfort as a trio was often told, "You guys are so good; you should get a guitar player!" They tried but couldn't find the right fit.

Pastor Greg Laurie referred to me as "Bullet Head" (think Spitzer bullet) due to my habit of blow-drying my hair and scrunching it up as high as possible along the part running down the middle. Greg was probably jealous. He had no hair to scrunch up.

Greg suggested that I audition to play on Saturday nights at Calvary Riverside. The gatekeeper of Saturday nights was Sweet Comfort's bassist, Kevin. He was a short grizzly bear of a guy with a flat nose. Kevin wanted me to jam with his brother Rick, who was tall, thin, and long haired with a prominent nose. Zero resemblance! They had seen me play with Psalm 150.

We set to playing loudly in Kevin's garage one night. We were musically wandering through some electric blues. Without any segue or introduction, Bryan showed up and began blithely playing another song. Bryan was short then. He still is. He had golden locks and blue-tinted glasses, so he was often mistaken for a girl from behind. He wasn't thrilled about that. So he exorcised his angst on an unfortunate spinet piano that probably pined* for the years it had been left unused in a Methodist church basement.

But Bryan sang as if he were ten feet tall, and the room fairly shook with a soulful sound that we were developing. Our misfit union produced an odd blend of Canned Heat boogie mixed with Elton John pop. Why was this working so well? Without officially learning the songs, I had filled the empty space in the former trio's sound. It was as if a missing puzzle piece had snapped into place. God was doing something!

Soon we were playing huge events at Disneyland and other parks. I had always wanted to play the Tomorrowland stage. Turns out, it was an oversized elevator that dropped us down into the bowels of the Magic Kingdom, where we might see Mickey Mouse taking off his head so the chain-smoking girl in the suit could light up.

By 1976, I was constantly on tour with Sweet Comfort. Kevin was adamant that we should make a record. The project was produced with $8,000 borrowed from Bryan's girlfriend!

I have no idea how much the Sweet Comfort album sold. No one did. There was a disconnect between band

---

* Sugar pine is often used in spinet pianos, along with light spruce…

and label. Maranatha was our Calvary Chapel label, but they didn't seem to want us. We thought we were pretty cool, but Maranatha was promoting itself as the "Praise record" label. They didn't promote Sweet C. We felt like a red-headed Riverside stepchild.

The record had been mixed by Jonathan David Brown in our absence. I'll never forget the horror of hearing a trombone solo on the final mix. Don't get me wrong—I used to play trombone in high school. I love trombone. In *marching band*. I imagine even hardcore Sweet C fans who love the first record would love to know: "What's the deal with the trombone?" It was just wrong.

We asked to leave the label. After all, the label had invested how much? Oh, that's right: zero dollars. A meeting was set with Chuck Fromm and Jimmy Kempner. They said, "If you leave us, you won't last two weeks. Your chances are slim and none."

The intended disparagement had an opposite effect. From then on, every time the band's van broke down by the side of the road, every time a promoter stiffed us, every time we wanted to quit, we recited "Slim and None" to each other. It kept us going for another decade. We were determined to make Fromm and Kempner eat their words.

We had the beginnings of a national following. After the name "Sweet Comfort" had been mistaken for a pillow brand in one too many motels, we added the qualifier "Band." Ralph Carmichael's Light Records signed us up. Ralph never forgot our names—he wrote them down on a napkin every time he met us! Ralph had white hair, big glasses, and a whiskbroom mustache. Remember Disney's Pinocchio? Ralph looked like Geppetto.

Light Records did something we had never seen before: they promoted the record. We had started our first recording sessions at Martinsound in Alhambra with engineer Jack Joseph Puig. With our freshly minted songs, we took up again with Jack flying the ship and Bob Wilson at the helm. It worked well. The band had learned the basic disciplines of recording on the first album. We were a little more professional the second time around.

As is often the case, the principal writer in the band (Bryan) had used up a year's worth of songs on the first album. Rock bands face "the sophomore curse"—after a debut album of songs that were slaved over, the powers that be tell you to be brilliant and write a follow-up record. Pronto.

Our drummer, Rick Thomson, was a song starter. So I became a song finisher. This gave us a fresh batch of tunes. We had "Good Feelin'" and "Got to Believe" and others. Producer Bob Wilson was flying high with his band Seawind. He wrote "Breakin' the Ice" for us. He auditioned Bryan, Rick, and me to sing it. I won. While I was learning the song in the studio, Bob said, "OK. We got it."

"What do mean, 'We got it'?"

"I wanted to get a *live* feel," Bob replied. The audition was the finished vocal. The only good thing about that vocal is that I could always sing it better live than on the record!

The *Breakin' the Ice* record has a fun vibe. Bob knew what he was about. I stayed by his elbow for the whole project. After the project was finished, he made an announcement: "We're mixing at Record Plant. But here's the thing—no one can come to the mix sessions!"

The band howled. "Why? Why?"

Bob said, "The drummer will want more drums ... the bassist will want more bass ... it just doesn't work! I have to mix the record with the big picture in mind!"

Bob Wilson called me the next day and gave me dates and location for mixing. "Wait," I said. "I thought the band wasn't allowed."

Bob said, "They're not. You are. They only listen to their own parts. I've been watching you. You listen to everything. I need you at the mix."

I was there. Mix sessions are impressive. All the Frankenstein knobs and meters get fired up in the laboratory. Mike Stone engineered. (Never saw him before or after.) I stayed by Bob's side, like Spock on Kirk. Once things were sounding fairly balanced, Bob would ask my opinion. Without exception, he took my advice. It was great. We mixed *Breakin'* in two evenings. I had seen a record through, from the first song written to the last song mixed. No trombone solos.

Playing guitar had been my first thing. Then I learned songwriting. Now I was taking producer lessons in the dark underbelly of Los Angeles. I loved the studio world.

Oh, by the way, our first album, *Sweet Comfort*, sold primarily on the West Coast. *Breakin' the Ice* made us nationwide, and sales for the first record shot up. There's your "slim and none."

Songstory Writer Tip: Listen to a song and follow only one part. For instance, listen to Bonham play with Zeppelin. Listen to only James Jamerson's bass on a song; only the backing vocals on Def Leppard; etc. Why? To learn about drum parts, bass parts, vocal sounds, keyboards, guitars. Listen to ambience, effects, outboard gear—everything. Let me ask you, what's the most important part of a record? (And the answer is…) *Every part is important.* Learn all you can from every musician, writer, singer, and sound tech you meet. It all comes in handy when you're ready to get serious. And when the deck is stacked against you and the sun refuses to shine, just remember: "Slim and None."

Songstory XI

From the Baptism to the Babbling Brook

Hear that lonesome whippoorwill;
he sounds too blue to fly.
The midnight train is whining low;
I'm so lonesome I could cry.
(Hank Williams)

And I'm living it out on the road,
where I've got so far to go.
(Bryan Duncan)

YOU KNOW WHY our tours met with so many misadventures? We didn't have MapQuest and cell phones! We were also kind of stupid. Here is another collection of road stories. If you enjoy reading it half as much as I enjoyed recalling it, it will be like an E coupon at Disneyland. Please put your tray tables up and your hands inside the vehicle at all times. Enjoy your rock 'n' roll tour down Songstory Memory Lane!

The Baptism

When I first joined Sweet Comfort Band, the first thing I learned about was "the baptism." Bassist Kevin

Thomson had been the beneficiary of an intestinal bypass. I suspect the doctors took out all the filters and inserted a silencer. Kevin was no small guy. My baptism occurred when we were rehearsing in Kevin's garage in Riverside. Suddenly, there was literally no oxygen in the room. I thought there had been a nuclear blast. Every molecule in the air had turned poisonous. Noxious methane.

Rick and Bryan laughed at my expression and assured me it was Kevin. "Can't be," I croaked. "Are you sure it's not anthrax?" We three breath-holding band members left unrepentant Kevin in his own green cloud and went to lunch (Naugle's) for an hour. When we returned, a menacing mist still lingered over Central Avenue.

Rehearsal was canceled.

As time went by, we had sound men, lighting guys, pastors, promoters, and sometimes whole audiences experience the "baptism." The first time we drove into Canada, it was freezing. (It's a sadistic Christian booking agency policy that you must tour Canada in the winter.) We pulled over in a twelve-passenger van with the engine on, heater going full blast. Kevin got out and crossed four lanes of traffic to go to a phone booth.

Some poor, unsuspecting Canuck waddled up and stood next to the booth, waiting to use the phone. Kevin must have let one fly. Oh, you should have seen the look on this confused Canadian's face! He toddled across the street in a daze, probably thinking international terrorists were gassing the border. Well, we were laughing across the four-lane boulevard until ... until it hit *us!* You think I'm exaggerating, but I have *four* witnesses!

The laughter turned to tears.

Imagine singing on stage. You go for that big breath before singing a high note—and with no warning: zero oxygen! Only deadly nerve gas! Your eyes swell while the throat constricts and instinctively goes into gag reflex! In auditoriums we would watch whole rows of our audience get up and leave! They would all be choking and pointing at each other, thinking it had to be someone right next to them.

Kevin would just smile.

Bryan predicted that all who traveled with Kevin would eventually die of some new form of cancer that would baffle scientists. All we could do was cultivate air circulation and avoid elevators at all costs. Our Sweet Comfort Band white bread truck could often be seen driving in sub-zero weather with all the doors and windows wide open. A swift current of uninfected air was the only defense.

The Baptism was like a silent atomic disturbance. Near ground zero, everything died immediately. It spread menacingly like a low-lying invisible fog, impervious to glass, brick, or metal. The experience could be traumatic with the benefit of distance, such as being in the fourth row of an auditorium. Stinging eyes, disorientation, nausea, and asphyxiation followed. The lack of close proximity enabled the olfactory glands to come under full attack. Never, ever light a match. And buy new clothes.

One day, the hellacious torture almost paid off. We were sitting at a Holiday Inn with a traveling Christian comedy troupe named Isaac Air Freight. They had a guy named Dave Toole. Their crew was bragging that Toole could clear a room. Bryan and I claimed that Kevin could clear a stadium. We offered any odds; we would feed Toole and Kevin chili and beans, and then we'd lock both of them in a hotel room. First one to break down the door would lose. We must have overplayed our hand, because they chickened out. Maybe it's not right to make money off of a baptism.

I'd like to apologize for exaggerating. I'd like to, but I can't! There is no exaggerating Kevin's odoriferous potency during those years. The fact that it lessened as time went on is proof that there is a God. The fact that it happened proves that God has a sense of humor.

Keaggy and the Powder

Sweet C. teamed with Phil Keaggy on some dates. There was a rumor that Jimi Hendrix said Keaggy was the greatest guitarist in the world. When I asked Phil, he didn't even let me finish the question. He denied it as an urban legend. Of course, hearing Phil play will help you understand the rumor. I had to play next to him on stage many times. It's a healthy lesson in humility.

I roomed with Phil. One morning, I woke up, and Phil was gone. He appeared later that morning. I saw him hunched in a corner, pouring white powder into a bag. He was mixing another powder with it. Was Phil out buying drugs? Oh, no…

During breakfast, Phil started sprinkling something on his food. Intrigued, I asked, "What's that?"

"Cayenne pepper and garlic!" Phil enthused. He held up the bag. "Want some?"

"No, thanks. Hey, where'd you go this morning?"

"Running. I run every morning!"

Thus ended the mystery of Phil Keaggy and the bag of powder.

Band Photo

In 1978 or so, Sweet Comfort Band stopped in a Marie Callender's restaurant in Sacramento. A promoter had given me a three-by-five-inch photo of the band as a memento. I showed it to the guys, who were duly unimpressed. We saw each other every day.

After lunch, I went into the men's room. There was no place to set the photo. So I stepped up to a urinal. I placed the photo between my teeth. Bryan came in and asked me a question. I answered. That was my mistake. The photo floated left to right like a feather until it came to rest on the red bullseye that covered the little drain, below the bathroom floor. There was nothing else I could do. So I kind of watered it.

I pointed it out to Bryan, who was "relieved" to have a target. We called in the whole band. Then the road crew. We left it there for strangers to desecrate. We had so many fans in that town that I always wondered if a customer came in that restroom to winky and recognized the long-haired Jesus Freaks in the urinal. Perhaps he thought,

Isn't that Sweet Comfort Band? Looks like someone really doesn't like them. Oh, well ... when in Rome...

Keith Green Quit the Record Business

We shared the stage with Keith Green in the late '70s. In Chicago, Keith announced that he was quitting the record business. His devoted fans were shocked. After the concert, I was having dinner with Keith.

"You're quitting the record business? What's that mean?"

"Well, I'm tired of record companies charging for the Gospel. No more records."

Keith did make a record. He offered it directly to his fans. That way, they wouldn't have to pay seven dollars for each copy. Sparrow record executive Peter York later told me that about 60,000 units were shipped for free. Over 200,000 were sent to customers who paid a free-will offering.

I asked, "How did that work out?"

Peter's face brightened. "The average offering has been twenty dollars!"

The Frozen Lock

Sweet C had an Italian sound man. His first name rhymes with Phil. Apparently, Phil had not traveled much in cold weather. It was around 1980. It was certainly winter, and probably in British Columbia. I remember we passed through an ominous tunnel that looked to be dripping thousands of blue icicles. A frozen road sign said, "Hell's Gate." I tried to take a photo. My camera shutter was frozen.

We were traveling in the UPS-style white van with a blue "Sweet Comfort Band" painted on the sides. Behind this was a white tandem trailer that was holding equipment. Securing the trailer was a chrome Master combination lock. The whole rig was decorated with icicles.

The heater had failed on our van. We were nearly frostbitten. Once we had arrived at the venue, the band rushed into the heated building and warmed ourselves. We asked for some local Canadians to go outside to help Phil unload the equipment. The band was hoping to get some feeling back in our fingers and toes.

The local Canadians came rushing back into the gym. Something was seriously wrong with Phil, and the combination lock. Not surprisingly, it was frozen.

We ran out to the trailer. There was poor Phil, yelling, "MMMMMMFH! MMMMMMMF! MMMMMMMM MMMMMMMMFFFFFFFFFFFHHHH!"

Apparently, Phil had tried to unfreeze the lock by breathing on it. When that didn't work, I guess he tried to ... well ... warm the metal lock ... with his *mouth!*

The whole episode was funny enough, until the locals implemented the plan to get Phil's mouth off of the frozen lock. Yep. They brought hot water out and poured it over Phil's head! It worked. But the water in the hair, beard, and jacket quickly turned to hard, cold ice.

Poor Phil looked like Jack Frost.

You're Making Me Sick

The first time Sweet Comfort Band was in New York City, it was a culture shock. The promoters had a NYC band opening for us. They took us to see the equipment they were lending to us. The gear was described with (how should I say this?) very colorful language. They used all the four-letter words that made us blush. After viewing the equipment, the guys in the band proudly assured us, "Good f***ing $#!t, huh?"

"Um. Yeah. Nice ... uh, thanks!"

We were taken to a greasy diner. This is normally something I would like. I noticed a cockroach rubbing his little front feet together while perched atop the grimy cash register. I quietly whispered this to my band members. The roach combed his antennae. The promoter heard me whispering. He bellowed, "What? What's the problem?" I pointed at the cockroach discreetly. He yelled out (the promoter yelled, not the cockroach), "Hey! One of youse wanna get rid of the cockroach here? You're making me SICK!"

The other customers kept eating. The dishwasher decided to dispatch the bug. He put down a plate he was drying and stretched out his wet towel. He pulled on one end and aimed at the cash register. THWAP! The roach was catapulted to another part of the kitchen. Presumed wounded in action. The dishwasher unfurled the towel and went back to drying dishes with it.

That night we played in a nineteenth-century New York City church building. I saw an amazing transformation: The band that had cussed like sailors during the day were transformed into Church People. The guitarist said, "Glory to God, we wanna praise the Lord tonight! Amen? Hallelujah!" Their speech had gone from worldly to saintly in a Big Apple second.

James talks about how our mouths can be like a well that brings both sweet water and bitter (James 3:11). James says these things ought not to be so. It was a stark example of Saturday night cussing versus Sunday morning pretense. Maybe I never heard that kind of language in California ... because we are sneakier than New Yorkers.

The Day the Music Didn't Die

Sweet Comfort Band had a lot of breakdowns in the '80s. We pushed a van made for bread deliveries for a half million miles, then horse-whipped a retired Greyhound bus past its designed capacity. Tires, fan belts, transmissions, engines—we blew anything that could be blown. We even drove to one gig holding a cracked windshield up against a snowstorm.

You know the cliché of the gas station mechanic charging ten times the fair price for engine work? Well, we met that guy in many a remote town. Long-haired hippies with a broken truck, in a hurry, with lots of T-shirt cash on hand, equals Suckers.

We were outside San Antonio. The engine was blown. The kind of blown where mechanics shake their heads and laugh as if to say, *Boy, are you stupid, and this is gonna cost ya.* We unloaded the equipment and began to pray for some way to get to our engagements.

May I interrupt myself for a moment? If I don't, my wife will.

In the early '90s, I was driving with my young son Randall at my side. A UPS truck whizzed by with the door open. That caused me to tell my son about the days when we had a white bread truck with Sweet Comfort Band painted on the side. I told him that we drove that thing so hard and long that we kept blowing motors. I said, "We must have put four engines in that truck!" He thought about that for a moment.

"Wow," he said. "Was it loud?"

Back to the laughing mechanics. We somehow got our skinny selves and a mound of gear to San Antonio. Then, we needed to get to Houston (a three-hour drive). Kevin Thomson was made for such emergencies. He found a private plane and an empty tractor-trailer. The other three band members grabbed the chance at a plane ride and were going to have a leisurely flight, while the crew and I had to hitch a ride in the 18-wheeler overland. I felt screwed.

There was a cheery young guy named Robin King who kindly volunteered to drive the 18-wheeler, since he owned a fleet of them. We put our equipment in the trailer. "That all you got?" It was like throwing a few rocks into the Grand Canyon. The sound guys bunked in the sleeper. I had the luxury of sitting shotgun. We started lumbering toward Houston. Robin was a very fun guy to travel with, and we became instant best friends while rolling along the Texas blacktop.

Meanwhile, unbeknownst (don't you love that word?) to me, Kevin, Rick, and Bryan were flying in a specially outfitted four-seater plane, since the pilot was a paraplegic. He was wheeled into the cockpit, and he worked the hand controls. They took off without a problem, but the further they flew, the more the pilot got disoriented. He became lost.

The pilot handed a map to Rick. "See if you can figure out where we are!" The map made no sense to Rick or the other guys. Look at a map; look at the ground. They began flying around in circles, looking for landmarks. Brother, you can fly around for a *long* time over Texas. And a lot of it just looks like more Texas.

Finally, Rick (who tends to take charge in a crisis) commanded, "Find a place to land! Now!" The pilot became more upset. He said something about being low on fuel.

At his passengers' insistence, the paraplegic pilot found an open field. He brought the plane down. Now, I didn't know that planes could bounce, but this guy *bounced* the plane like a basketball! BAM! Bryan and the brothers were praying that today was not the day they were appointed to die (Hebrews 9:27). They all had wives and children. They really wanted to see them again. The pilot made another landing effort. BAM! This time the craft bounced like a Christian promoter's check!

Their hearts sunk. On that second BAM, the pilot did something that a pilot should never, ever do: He passed out.

The Sweet C guys were screaming and shaking the pilot, to no avail. Rick took over the hand controls. What do you do? Rick lowered the wheel. The plane lost altitude. It was Rick's first moment flying, and now four lives depended on his flying skills. The ground came up slowly under the aircraft. They were headed for some tall weeds. The weeds began brushing the underbelly.

Rick tried to set that bird down easily. There was a swishing sound. One wheel, and then the other touched down. The nose went up. Rick was stomping. "Where are the brakes on this thing?" The plane shuddered and acted as if the brakes had been applied. Was it a miracle? All they could see now was blue skies as green reeds rushed by. The little plane came to a slow roll, then stopped. The engine hissed and steamed like a locomotive.

They were unharmed.

Grass was growing through water all around them. It was knee deep. Yep. Rick had set her down in a Texas-sized mud puddle! Where were they? How did they get the unconscious pilot out of the swamp? How did they make their way to Houston? I don't know all the specifics. They say necessity is the mother of let's-get-the-flock outta here.

Meanwhile in Houston, an audience had shown up, but the band had not. I went out to face the crowd. I defaulted to playing some worship songs. I was leaning heavily on the Holy Spirit, which is good. About the time that my ad-libbed one-man show was beginning to wear thin, the back door opened. Down the aisle came Rick, Kevin, and Bryan. Their shoes made a sloshing sound. Their pants were still wet. They looked none too happy.

It was the shortest concert that SCB ever did. The sound guys and I were rested and happy. The three soggy survivors were not in the mood to smile or do anything other than play a few numbers and talk about how tonight may be the last night we have to live. Let that serve as a lesson. You can accept Jesus. Or go to hell.

They had narrowly averted a muddy death. You might think they would be happy to be on the ground. Nope. They were still mad! Worst. Day. Ever.

Me? I had dinner plans with my new best friend Robin. One of the *best* days ever! The moral is—the best revenge is to not be in a plane crash.

Under Arrest

The Cruse Family was an actual Texas family headed by father/pastor Joe Cruse. Joe liked to recruit anyone who married into the family into his band. I learned this from Jeff Adams, who ran sound and drove the bus for them. That's what you get for not playing an instrument. I was walking by a table at a Christian festival when father/pastor Joe stood up and grabbed me. I mean, it was like being under arrest.

"I heard you playing and singing out there; impressive; you're a Christian, right?"

"Yes, sir." I always say "sir" when someone has a bear grip on my arm.

"You play other instruments, son?"

"Well, yes, bass, drums, and…"

"You ever drive a bus?"

"Uh, yes…"

Joe's grip tightened, if that were possible. "You married?"

"No…"

Joe put his arm around me. "You ever met my daughter Cindy?"

Held for Questioning

In the '70s, SCB worked with the Billy Graham organization. We entered Canada just below Vancouver, B.C. We were issued work visas in order to play in Canada. The customs agents seemed to take American bands as a threat.

"So, why aren't you yoosing Canadian musicians, eh?"

We would answer, "Well, we come from southern California and play original music. If you had Canadian musicians and singers playing our music, it wouldn't be the real thing, would it? Wouldn't that be a cover band? You could boycott American bands, I suppose. But that cuts both ways. Would you want Canadian music to be kept out of the U.S.? That would probably be the end of Canadian music…"

They didn't like that answer.

After a Vancouver concert, Sweet C. was scheduled to drive overnight into Alberta. Kevin asked customs agents specifically how we could drive into Alberta and play the concert on schedule. (It was a twelve-hour drive! Soooo, that's like a long way, eh?) We were advised to drive to Calgary and get our work visa the day after. So, technically we played a concert on a Saturday night and came into Alberta customs as instructed on a Sunday.

Kevin dutifully drove us to the customs office and explained that we had played a concert the night before. You would have thought we had confessed to torturing Canada geese. The band was brought into the office. The truck was searched. We were separated and questioned Gestapo-style. They began threatening us with deportation.

I heard Bryan getting angry in another room. Customs agents are like mall cops. They desperately need to feel like big shots. These blue-suited Barney Fifes were getting really worked up. We kept saying, "We were following instructions. We haven't done anything wrong. If you want to deport us, deport us." (Anything to end the Fifing.)

This was in the days of Long Hair = Drug Dealer. Thankfully, the power-hungry boys in blue got a phone call from the States. Apparently, our holdup had gotten to Dr. Billy Graham. He had called customs and vouched for our little band. He must have talked to the Top Fife. The tone reversed. We were released with red-faced apologies. (OK, so good day, eh?)

For decades after that incident, every time I came into Canada, I was pulled aside by more than one agent. Why? Because their records showed that I had been "HELD FOR QUESTIONING" (which looks to them like drugs were involved). Paul Brandt band saw it years later. Then with SHeDaisy. It happened with Shania every time. Still to this day (thanks to computers), they look at me like I'm an ex-con.

The agent will look at a computer screen. Then he will whisper something to another agent. They both stare at the screen. Then one will say, "OK, so, Mr. Thomas, so, have you ever been like, held for questioning?" They are hoping I'll deny it.

"Yes!" I say. "I once played a concert in Alberta before acquiring a work visa. Boy, I'll never make that mistake again. Those Calgary agents really play by the book!" They usually accept that explanation.

But they still eye me with suspicion.

Ooh, It's the Spirit

Drummer Rick had lost his front teeth in a fist fight. Very rock 'n' roll. So he had front dentures made. He used to come out from behind the drums and play acoustic guitar. Rick's hair would get caught in the strings. So, he would fling his hair behind his back.

One night in the mid-'70s, Sweet Comfort was playing The Warehouse, a mega-church in Sacramento. Rick came out to sing, "Ooh, It's the Spirit." But this night the first chorus started (and ended) with "Ooh, it's the *FOOOMPH!*"

The teeth flew out into the audience.

Rick jumped out after it. Song over. Bryan said, "It's the first stage-diving I had ever seen!" For some reason, we didn't play the song after that.

Lost Backstage

There were multiple occasions when we got lost backstage. Go check out the scene in *Spinal Tap*. I think they wrote that scene after they heard about us. My favorite occasion was with Bryan Duncan. We got lost in the catacombs of some arena. Finally, we found a door labeled Stage Door. "Oh, praise the Lord!"

We burst in. The concert was ready to begin. The audience all had white hair. A goateed man stood ready to take the stage. We asked, "Are we in the right place?"

The familiar-looking man said, "You're in the right place if you're ready to sing along!"

(Someone said, "They're ready for you, Mr. Miller.")

"Sing along with what?"

"Sing along with Mitch!"*

---

* If you were born after 1960, you may have to Google *Sing Along with Mitch*. Then, take my word for it—that was funny in 1978. Mitch Miller was singing oldies to counter all that rock 'n' roll that nobody really likes. Mitch said of rock, "It's not music. It's a disease."

They Tell Me I Had a Good Time

In 1983, Sweet Comfort appeared on a bill with Tom Johnston (who sang many of the early Doobie Brothers' hits) and Three Dog Night at Mammoth Ski Resort. Three Dog had all original members. I was impressed. After the show, the three singers were flown out by helicopter. This was my chance to hang out with guitarist Michael Allsup for a minute. He was sitting on a road case with nothing to do. I introduced myself.

After some guitarist trade-talk, I asked, "So, how crazy was it in the '70s? You must have some great stories!"

He shrugged. "I was doing so many drugs back then. To be honest, I don't remember anything."

That was the end of the conversation. After we shook hands and I was leaving, Michael called out apologetically, "They tell me I had a good time!"

The Babbling Brook

I avoid saying, "God told me." I try to quote the Bible in a responsible way. But God has whispered to me on a couple of occasions. The most significant of these was in Medford, Oregon. It was 1978. Sweet Comfort Band was on tour. For some reason, I had hours to kill. I was outside a church. I wandered off into a wooded area.

I must have been praying profusely. I say that, because I prayed myself "out." I said so much that was on my mind that I reached the end of my blathering. But I kept the line open. A little babbling brook seemed to invite me to sit down and shut up.

I had an odd premonition that something was coming. If I would just remain quiet, it would come. It's hard to explain. I entered into a state of prayer that was like pure Waiting. Listening. With each passing second, the babble of the world went further away until it seemed to no longer exist. The bank of that creek became holy ground.

A still small voice came to my thoughts. It was certainly not audible, but there seemed to be a need for a clearing of thoughts before it could arrive. (I'm writing down my description just in case it is helpful to someone, or if someone else has had a similar experience.) It was very deliberate and distinct. Here is what I heard:

Before you were in the womb, I knew you.
Before you were born, I set you apart.
I watched you grow. I was with you, even though you were unaware of My Presence. I knew you before you knew Me. I have always known you.
No eye has seen and no ear has heard, nor has anyone imagined the place I have prepared for you!
Right now you can only see Me as though looking through a dark glass. But one day you will see Me face to face. You will know Me as I have known you.

There was a pause.

But as for now, I love you just as you are.

That last sentence sent me into joyful weeping. In the years since this happened, I have recounted this experience to only a few people. (I'm a Presbyterian, after all.) With benefit of hindsight analysis, I see the form was Past/Future/Present. It is interesting that the more Bible I learn, the more the whisper resonates with God's Word. From He who was, and is, and is to come.

Consider the following scriptures: "Before I formed you in the womb I knew you, before you were born I set you apart" (Jeremiah 1:5). "We love because he first loved us" (1 John 4:19). "I go to prepare a place for you" (John 14:2). "For now we see in a mirror dimly, but then face to face. Now I know in part; then I shall know fully, even as I have been fully known" (1 Corinthians 13:12). "And after the earthquake a fire, but the Lord was not in the fire. And after the fire the sound of a low whisper" (1 Kings 19:12). "What no eye has seen, nor ear heard, nor the heart of man imagined, what God has prepared for those who love him" (1 Corinthians 2:9). "But God shows his love for us in that while we were still sinners, Christ died for us" (Romans 5:8).

I don't know what God wants you to do, but I hope you know that He knew you before you were born. He always watches out for you. He has heavenly plans for you. And because of Christ, He loves you as if you were His only child.

We walk through the valley of the shadows. They say the valley is where the fruit grows. For me, these "still small voice" occasions have been rare. I don't think you can drum them up. I rely on God's Word and the Holy Spirit, not on experiences, because feelings are fleeting.

But I'll never forget those words being whispered to me.

I'm glad I sat by the babbling brook that night.

Songstory Writer Tip: The easiest songs are the ones that curl up in your lap. Most of the time, I suggest you write like a craftsman—work at it with tools. But there are exceptions. You may wake up in the morning with a song in your skull. Or you overhear a conversation and it sparks a song. Try to develop your songwriter "antennae."

On a good day, you might hear a song blowing in the wind. Songs are not actually floating out there in the ether—but human creativity is a powerful force. Listen for the whisper. My guess is that this will work only on rare occasions. It's great when it does. What is more common is working with a co-writer and he plays you something. When he comes to a dead end, you might hear the next section. It will come to you.

On the other occasions, go through your list of prepared titles, mess around with some music, and get back to work. The whisper may come tomorrow.

Songstory XII

Cricket with an Attitude

I was born with music inside me.
Music was one of my parts.
Like my ribs, my kidneys, my liver, my heart.
Like my blood.
It was a force already within me
when I arrived on the scene.
It was a necessity for me—like food or water.
(Ray Charles)

When does life ever turn out like you imagined?
(Songstory)

AFTER TWO STELLAR album covers, the third SCB cover looked like Rocky and Bullwinkle were now running the art department. I didn't even like the title (*Hold on Tight!* 1980). This was the first time the band did not have creative control. The music was a yawn to me. The band was performing well. Yet, I would say this was our "sophomore curse" project. The songs sounded like someone announced, "Boys, we need to write songs for the next record! Think of a snappy title that looks good on T-shirts!"

Touring in those days was haphazard. Saturday might be a huge festival, followed by Sunday in a coffee house. This might be followed by a night in a Christian commune, and then a long drive to a church that was convinced that rock 'n' roll was Devil Music. Our favorite venues were high schools and colleges where we encountered non-Christians. This is where Kevin did his thing best: he talked about Jesus in everyday language. At nearly every concert, we saw dozens of converts.

The Blues Brothers claimed to be on a "mission from God." SCB claimed it, too. Only we were serious.

Hearts of Fire

The next record from this traveling salvation show was *Hearts of Fire* (1981). We were back to our usual great SCB cover art. There were four armored star troopers on the front, slaying a dragon. We incorporated a ringer on this outing. John Schreiner played keys and did some great chordal twists. It kicked us into a higher gear. He was our Billy Preston/fifth Beatle. I wrote and sang my first solo-ish outing, "Just Like Me," which became an oft-used wedding song.

All of these records involved Jack Joseph Puig capturing the sound. Jack became the super-sought-after L.A. engineer. If you look up the word "intense," you should see a picture of Jack. He would get us into the hottest studios and show up in a classic Porsche with two-inch tapes strapped into the passenger seat.

While recording vocals at Mama Jo's in North Hollywood, we encountered a cricket hidden in the studio wall. We couldn't find it or get it to shut up. We were doing sensitive backing vocals on "Just Like Me."

Bryan suggested we record anyway, rather than call the session off. I said, "If you can't beat 'em, multitrack 'em!" We recorded the cricket by himself on multiple takes, so we had a believable background of crickets on the song.

This was probably a mistake. The next day, when we returned, the cricket was wearing a beret and shades. He was demanding songwriting credit and wanted to be paid triple scale.

Cutting Edge

Cutting Edge (1982) was a good follow-up to *Hearts of Fire*. It bugged me that we had no title song, so I slipped the album title into my lyrics. I was writing complete songs either alone or committee-style with band members. I woke up one morning and heard the complete song "Valerie" in my head. (As usual, the lyrics took some work.) "Falling in Love with You" is a favorite.

John Schreiner made a huge contribution to introductions and arrangements. John worried us. He would show up late saying things like "I totaled my car on the way here" or "I slept on a park bench last night." He had a genius/savant thing going.

Rick and I were recording one night (on an outside project) with the very talented Howard McCrary. Howard had recorded vocals with Michael Jackson. We were in a studio somewhere south of Los Angeles. Jack Puig called us. "I'm in the studio with the Toto guys, working on a Brothers Johnson record. You guys need to come and hear this!" The problem was, it was past midnight.

Rick called his wife. He suggested to Howard, "You should call your wife and get permission to stay out that late. We might not get home until dawn…"

Howard said, "I don't need to ask my wife anything."

Rick insisted. "Are you sure?"

Howard said, "Watch this!" He picked up the studio phone and called his wife. It was like a Bob Newhart comedy routine, since all we heard was one side of the conversation:

"Hello, baby … I was just … no …wait … but … I'm here with the Sweet Comfort … no, hold on … they invited me to go to a studio in North Holly— … well … but if … now, just … yeah, but … I know … could … we were gonna … no … yeah, but … you don't …honey, if I could … no, I didn't … but if … yes, I do know what time it … uh huh …no, I didn't mean it like … OK … no, yeah … OK … you're right, but … all right … I'm sorry … oh … OK…"

His wife kept talking. Howard hung his head. "I'll be right home, baby."

Rick and I went to watch Toto pull an all-nighter in the studio … without Howard.

Bob-Bep-Poo

Drummer Rick used to get tired while thrashing away behind the band. One night, he decided to end the concert. He thought, *If I just call out, "Goodnight!" the concert will be over.* He grabbed the mic at the end of a song. Just before he said goodnight, he thought,

Maybe I should say, "God bless you." His exhausted brain short-circuited. What came out was "BOB-BEP-POO!" After that, SCB ended every gig with "BOB-BEP-POO!" Some traditions are just worth it.

Perfect Timing

On *Perfect Timing* (1983), we broke with form. The band was wooed by the Elefante brothers. Jack Joseph Puig had no contract with us, but I assume our change in engineers upset him; he never talked to us again.

There was a ticking time bomb in the band: Bryan and I needed some semblance of say in the business. Kevin and Rick had been running the show. Personally, I was on the low end of the band pay scale with zero control over the band agenda. Bryan and I were growing artistically, but we were having no say in the decisions.

Take a look at Bryan's titles: "Habit of Hate." "Envy and Jealousy." Bryan always wrote from personal experience. I accidentally came up with the album title. One day I returned home from a tour. Just as I unlocked and opened the door, the phone rang. I'd been gone for weeks! How did the caller know I just walked in? I set down my luggage and answered the phone: "Perfect Timing!" I don't remember who was calling. I ran to grab a guitar and wrote the song. As it developed, Perfect Timing became an interesting theme for a break-up record.

Dino sensed the tension in the band. He probably should have treaded carefully. Instead, he threw fuel on the fire. He encouraged Bryan to go solo. He talked with me about starting another band. He was the Yoko to our Beatles!

Sweet Comfort Band fell apart during that project. Bryan and I (foolishly) wanted out as soon as possible. Ray Ware, acting as our agent, insisted we honor our performance agreements. A deal was struck: Ten final Sweet Comfort Band dates were booked. The four band members would be paid equally. Rick and Kevin could keep all of the merchandising monies. *Perfect Timing* would be finished.

It was not an ideal environment to finish a project. But we were merely tired of each other; there was nothing close to a fist fight (which would be very rock 'n' roll). Bryan and I were setting our sights on future freedom. We finished the recording. Thanks to John Elefante's soaring backing vocals, the record sounds a lot like Kansas.

The final *Perfect Timing* tour saw the band divided into two factions: the Leavers and the Left. But shifting the finances into a four-way split was rewarding. For those ten concerts, I was paid ten *thousand* dollars. You read that right! That's with four zeros! I became a thousandaire! The last farewell date was in the hometown of Riverside, California. Steve Camp opened.

After the final concert, I think Bryan felt liberated. I was nervous but ready to move on. Rick had a new business going. But Kevin had spent twelve years working tirelessly for the band. He had invested his soul into Sweet Comfort Band. Kevin cried.

Sweet ALLIES

We were offered a Sweet Comfort Band European tour. We would have loved to have done an ALLIES tour, but nobody had heard of the band yet. The crazy idea emerged of having Rick and Kevin of SCB join Bob and Sam of ALLIES, with me as a common denominator. I made it clear that this was a one-off. Then we would launch ALLIES.

SCB without Bryan? Would that work? Europe had never seen Sweet Comfort Band. Ray Ware was not gruntled. He was disgruntled. Ray asked Bryan, "They can't make that work! Bob can't sing as well as you, can he?"

Bryan replied, "Yes, Ray. Bob can sing as well as anybody!"

It's a major adjustment swapping out lead singers. Bob showed his versatility by covering Bryan's vocal parts in his own style. It was a band between two worlds for me. Rick and Kevin were a different side of a musical coin from Sam and Bob. Looking back, the tour was not the best of ideas nor the worst. But—it was EUROPE! It was a final gasp for Sweet C., and it paved the way for ALLIES.

I played some guitar tracks on Bryan's solo records. Bryan and I also communicated on the preparation of SCB *Prime Time* (1985). It had a reasonably good cover. There's a tradition that when a band breaks up, the label must release a "best of." Have you ever done a Best Of? It's a sign your career is over.

Decades later, the Sweet Comfort Band records were reissued. Have you ever had a record reissued? It's a sign that you are old.

The Waiting Is Over

Speaking of old, I'd like to fast forward about twenty-seven years. By 2009, Kevin was having serious health issues. We got the band back together in Rick's Shelter Studios. Our songwriting muscles were still in great shape. Things progressed slowly. We were all so busy. Rick and Bryan were still in the Riverside, California, area. I was the SCB guy who left California for Nashville for Florida.

Rick and Bryan came up with a title song: "The Waiting Is Over." There were 400 long years of silence between the Old Testament and the New. The band felt as if it had been 400 years since we had put a record out. Plus, the progress was about as slow as a turtle in mud. Kevin came to a session in a motorized wheelchair. He took me aside and said, "I have one request. If the band ever plays, and I'm not around, have Josh and Eli play. OK?"

Kevin reiterated, "Promise me, OK?"

I said, "Sure, Kevin." That was the last time I saw him.

The family arranged a memorial at Calvary Chapel in Costa Mesa, the old Papa Chuck home base. Josh and Eli came to play with the band. None of this was how I pictured it (playing without Kev). When does life ever turn out like you imagined?

We loaded in through the familiar Calvary back door. I felt like I'd played there a thousand times. There was a long hallway behind the platform that acted as a "backstage." I thought of the days when Love Song, Children of the Day, Second Chapter, and Keith Green hung out in there. I wondered whatever happened to the pants-less guy who gave his grey bell-bottoms for the cause of Bob Carlisle. (See the Exploding Pants story...)

At the far end of that hall, a guy was blow-drying his white hair. He looked like Darrell Mansfield. I thought maybe I was having a flashback. Darrell was one of the faces that used to haunt this hallowed hall.

Sweet Comfort Band played the memorial service. Kevin's wife Robin was there. Behind me was Rick on drums. Eli on bass. Josh next to me. Bryan on my left. Rob Rinderer on keys. Behind them was ... Darrell Mansfield. Playing harmonica.

Wait.

What? Why was Darrell Mansfield there?

I sat with my wife as eulogies were given. I wept. For the first time, maybe I understood why Jesus wept. I wasn't sad for Kevin—he was in the presence of the Lord, where there is inexpressible joy (Psalm 16:11). But there is such sadness for those who don't place their faith in the one who is the resurrection and the life (John 11:25). Death is the enemy.

On the drive back toward the Inland Empire, Rick, Bryan, and I sat in silence. Something was nagging at us. I said, "Um, who invited Darrell Mansfield?"

Rick said, "I didn't. Did you, Bryan?" Bryan shook his head.

Again there was a stretch of quiet, when no one knew what to say. Anger began to build. Rick clenched his teeth. "He crashed our funeral…"

Bryan banged on the dashboard and yelled, "HE CRASHED OUR FUNERAL!"

We still had a record to finish. It became our Slim and None tribute to Kevin. Joshua and Elijah played on the record.

I tried to write a song about Kevin. Writing autobiographically works for Bryan, but it works against me. It was difficult. Lori had to help me. You can't just write "My friend Kevin died, and now I'm sad." After some fits and starts, the song came. It needed the ray of hope. It needed tears of joy in the mix.

Elijah produced me as I sang "In the Light of Heaven" about his dad.

Bryan really brought the vocal magic to the project. Rick broadened his playing to fit in between the old style and the new century. Bob Carlisle contributed creamy backing vocals. I did a solo on "Something Else Is Going on Here." I played it in my pajamas at home. I bet you didn't know that. Or want to. Elijah channeled his father's playing and took it beyond anything I've ever heard.

By 2012, Rick had worked on a cover and compiled all our work. Rick and his wife Alice dedicated a part of their lives to the seemingly endless process. *The Waiting Is Over* is Sweet Comfort Band's best record, in my opinion. Why? Probably because seasoned songwriters really have something to say.

Songstory Writer Tip: Some writers believe that they can write only when the muse strikes. Those are the kind of writers known as *amateurs*. Professionals will eventually be called on to write for a movie, a commercial, or some other project. I once had a paying client that asked me to write a song that was patriotic, that sounded like a truck rolling down the highway, that had girl singers. The title had to be "Texas Steel and Supply." I wrote it. The commercial got played. I got paid.

Listen to McCartney's "Live and Let Die." They asked him to write a Bond movie song. This shows you how a writer can switch from writing "what he feels like" to writing with the opening credits of a film in mind. It is seriously great.

You can write a song for somebody else's purposes sometimes. It feels a bit left-footed. But a pro can do it. In my experience, the muse appreciates a deadline. Try writing short jingles and commercial ditties. It's hard work. You might feel like a sellout, but you're not. You're not selling your soul, just a song. Plus, if you can do that kind of writing, you can pay for the equipment to record your own darling creations.

Songstory XIV*

Never Bite a Gift Horse in the Face

In the sweetness of friendship let there be laughter,
for in the dew of little things the heart finds
its morning and is refreshed.
(Khalil Gibran)

If I had it to do all over again, I wouldn't have the energy.
(Songstory)

A FAREWELL TOUR is the rock 'n' roll version of a lawn sale after a divorce. In 1983, Sweet Comfort Band did the ten goodbye concerts. Those were the days when farewell actually meant farewell. (Now it means "farewell until we need more money.") Christian media asked, "Why is SCB breaking up?" And the answer from me was that SCB ran its course, but we needed to move on. What now? The lead singer goes solo, of course. The guitar player starts another band.

---

* Where's Chapter XIII? Ever notice that many buildings don't have a thirteenth floor? That's just silly superstition. Ever notice that the Titans win every time I show up at the stadium wearing blue socks? That's not superstition. That's a *fact*. Nevertheless, in case the reader suffers from triskaidekaphobia, we skipped from chapter XII to XIV (that's 12 to 14 for those who don't speak ancient Roman). Don't expect a discount off of the price, though.

I had a band name: ALLIES. I created Art Deco logos on yellow legal pads, and I prayed. I tried starting the band with a few L.A. guys. It didn't work. I had too many preconceived ideas. In the '80s, most musicians were more concerned with hairstyle than content.

Sam Scott showed up on my doorstep. "I moved back from Holland! I heard Sweet C is ending. We should start a band..."

I was open. "That's something I'm praying about. I've got a name: ALLIES. Maybe that would work with getting a bunch of our old buddies together."

"Great. I know who the singer will be: Bob Carlisle."

"Really? Is Bob available?"

Sam and I went to see Bob fronting a band at a club called Rosie's in Rosemead, California. Bob was stellar. The club crowd had no idea how great he was. It turned out that Bob was ready to do anything to get out of "Club World." It was a dead end.

We set a meeting. Sam, Bob, and I gathered at Bob's house. I had a name, a vision, a song ("Morning Star"), and potential record contract. Sam had been leading his own band in Holland. I knew that Sam could write music. I knew Bob could sing better than anyone I'd ever heard in the studio—and he could tear it up live. We didn't know if Bob could write songs.

Bob's big question was, "Are we going to be a ministry, or are we going to be a band that makes enough money to feed my family?"

My answer was "Yes."

So ALLIES began that night. Sam and I started pitching in tunes. Bob had a girl-chasing song. The title was "Surrender." Kind of a racy idea. I wrote a new set of lyrics to Bob's music. It was a little strange at first. Bob had to adjust. My lyrics weren't spectacular, but it gave me chills to hear Bob sing it. We had our first number-one single written.

Sam had a song, "I'll Be Your Brother." A theme was coming together. Allies, surrender, brotherhood—all tied in well with a military theme. I arranged to have the phone number 8-ALLIES. We had army-style business cards made that looked like something from *M.A.S.H.* Everything had a military motif.

We recorded a demo of songs to seal the deal with Light Records. Gary Whitlock was my A&R buddy. Gary and I negotiated a contract in an unusually friendly fashion. When we went to ink the deal, I asked Gary how he liked the demo. He said, "Oh, I haven't heard it yet!" What an odd way to get a record deal—songs unheard!

Our first photo shoot was in front of a historic Los Angeles building. We sat on the sidewalk, backs to the outside wall. Bob felt something land on his head and ooze down his scalp. I looked up. Above us were a handful of pigeons perched with their butt ends hanging off the historic roof. Yep. Bob got pigeon bombed.

We added the taciturn Jim Erickson (drums) and the affable Matthew Chapman (bass) to the band. Jim is a technically astounding drummer. Matthew is an astoundingly lovable soul. This tied in our Psalm 150 and Sonrise heritage and made for an uncompromisingly great band. If Sweet Comfort Band had the strength of being an odd mix, this band had the strength of being homeboys who knew how to cut a deep groove.

Bob, Sam, and I were the writers/owners/leaders. Is it possible to have three leaders? Sort of. We divided responsibilities. I took on relations with booking, management, and record companies. Sam took touring details and traveling nightmares. Bob set up the concessions cash cow in his garage.

The first album cover shot was a faked ALLIES landing. If you look closely, you can see that Jimmy's face was pasted in from a different shot (a 1980s version of Photoshop). They silk-screened colors onto an enlarged photo. It has a campy comic-book appearance.

Trinity Broadcasting (TBN) did a video for "Surrender." It was meant to be WW2-era scratchy black and white. We staged a Normandy-style landing on Huntington Beach! Matt Crouch wanted to get a close-up of Bob singing. Matt ran forward with the camera and smacked Bob in the mouth. Between a fat lip and pigeon poop, Bob was paying a price to promote this band.

YouTube Alert: There is a video posted online with shots of Bob with a live fish in his mouth, and dolphins playing. This was inserted while the band performed at Sea World. *This is not part of the original video.* But Bob was willing to bite a fish to entertain!

The first ALLIES concert laid an egg. On Laguna Beach. But an unbelievably gorgeous blond girl came to see it. Her name was Lori. Lori watched us roll up to the venue in a tank. The band dropped down to the ground, dressed in full battle gear. We were ready to answer the media's questions and take photos. There was one guy. He didn't have any questions. Then we performed loudly for a tiny audience consisting of the promoter, Lori, and the record company rep.

Afterwards, I told Lori I used to be in a band that played for thousands of people. Yep. The first time Lori met me, she thought, "Aw, poor little buddy—he thinks he used to be somebody."

The first tour was with Joe English, formerly with Paul McCartney and Wings. It was the ALLIES Invasion Tour. We felt sorry that we were playing for Joe's audience, with him opening. Joe had a great band. His career was on a downward trend and ALLIES was on the way up. (As Bob would say, "We scratched and clawed all the way to the *middle!*")

Later we would learn that Joe had been hiding a drug habit. We were all so poor in those days, I don't know how Joe could keep himself messed up. If Joe English had been in the limelight more, there would have been a big scandal. He later got involved with a super legalistic church. That was strange, but it got Joe clean.

FAME Agency booking agent Mike Cavale gave us a fat notebook full of itineraries and contracts. Down on the list, we saw the venue: the Bronco Bowl. The band was so excited about this! Wow, a stadium! The Bronco Bowl! On our first tour! We counted the days until we drove to Dallas to play the Bronco Bowl stadium. When we drove up, all we found was a bowling alley. This can't be right. But it was the correct address. Then it hit us:

There is no such team as the Dallas Broncos.

We toured with Amy Grant. Well, sort of. While doing a bookstore appearance, we found a life-sized Amy Grant *Unguarded* stand-up poster in a back room. "Can we have it?"

"Sure!"

From then on, Amy came with us on stage. Bob would give her a big introduction. We would interact and "rock" with Amy for the rest of the set. Backstage, she never said a word to us. I mean, what a snob.

She stayed in Bob's room, so that was really scandalous. We felt guilty about this, but Amy was too cheap to get her own room. Finally, Amy's attitude led to a parting of the ways. American Airlines wouldn't let us put Amy in the overhead bins. She wouldn't pay for a ticket. Kept giving us the silent treatment. So we left her standing on an Atlanta airport tarmac. We hated to lose the "star power" of bringing her out on stage, but enough is enough. Some people.

Opening for Rez Band was a treat. They came to preach the Gospel. Loudly. There was no posturing or ego trips. Their crew took a liking to us. "Surrender" was our closing song, which ended with a dramatic *bam bam bam bam bam bam ... (long pause) ... BAM!* (Applause!)

One particular evening, the lighting guys rigged pyro (explosives, really) to go off on the last BAM of our opening set. The materials used looked like blocks of wood with two nails attached to wires. Between the wires, they poured a high explosive that looked like gunpowder (which it may have been).

The Rez crew was being generous. They wanted a big explosion on that final BAM. The band was confidently bringing our raucous set to the spread-legged, arms-raised, glorious climax. Nearing the big finale the moment came: *bam bam bam bam bam bam ... (long pause) ... KABOOOOOOOOOOOOM!*

Concurrent with the impressive explosion was a blinding flash of light. The audience caught the unforgettable sight of five military-garbed musicians cowering in fright with the facial expressions of men who had very likely soiled themselves!

We toured with Mylon and Broken Heart. We loved the band members and the crew. Bob and I could never figure Mylon out. We got a couple of long lectures from him, as he wore Elvis shades in a dark room. It was as if he spoke English but came from another planet. I'd ask Bob, "What was that about?"

And Bob would sigh, "I have no idea."

For years, I saw Mylon at the big Christian events. He always said to me, "Brother, I don't remember your name, but I love you." After seeing me play on stage a bunch of times, Mylon called me to a private meeting.

"Brother, I don't remember your name, but I love you. Brother, you're a great git-tar player. And brother, God is telling me you're gonna play guitar with me."

I said, "God doesn't make much sense, does He?"

Mylon drawled, "What do you mean, brother?"

I did a facial shrug. "God's telling you I'm going to play guitar with you, yet after two years you still don't know my name. Why didn't He didn't bother to tell you?"

After touring the debut record, we recorded the album *Virtues*. I felt it had the sophomore curse. Bob and Sam consider it their favorite. I guess I'm the odd guy out. "Somebody Told Me You Were Crying" was a favorite, though. You can hear the unborn "Butterfly Kisses" in Bob's vocal.

This was the year when Sam left the band. Promoters heard rumors that ALLIES was over. Matthew found out that the rumors came from Sam. This is the type of news that travels. It hurt more than our feelings. The year 1987 was a serious low point for the band. We had no record contract, no booking agency. Lori and I were newlyweds who were behind on our mortgage for the first time in our marriage. The band could have folded. Except that God always has a big but: But God had other plans.

Bob called me. "Wanna start a band?"

I laughed. "I think we already have one."

"Yeah? Well, what if we jump-start the band again, and you and I become the songwriter team? Like Steinberg and Kelly." (Bob's friends Billy Steinberg and Tom Kelly were writing the big pop hits of the day.)

"Okay. Deal."

Thus began Carlisle and Thomasongs, an ASCAP publishing company for the new songwriting team of Bob and Randy. We would aspire to be like Leiber and Stoller; Goffin and King; Lennon and McCartney! I upgraded my home eight-track rig to sixteen tracks. Bob and I wrote and recorded material, hoping that the demos would be listened to this time. We needed to land a record deal again.

And land it, we did. We flew with manager Ray Ware to Nashville. Ray was great at putting deals together. But he mangled some clichés: "Don't jump for the moon. You can't bite a gift horse in the face."

Even after jumping for the moon, ALLIES signed with Word Records label Dayspring. I proposed that the label let me record at my house in Redlands, California, using the album budget to buy gear. Neal Joseph was the label head. He asked, "Will it sound even better than these demos?"

"Of course!" we said. This time it was the demos that got us funded.

Bob and I were now in the studio business. At the risk of biting a gift horse in the face, we converted my garage and carport into ALLIES Recording Studio! We purchased a hot-rodded 3M 24-track machine from Hank Sanicola at O'Henry Studio in Burbank. We dubbed it Barney. Next was a smaller matching 3M two-track for mixing. She was named Betty. Our sound guy/studio buddy was Fred Tedesco. Fred, Barney, and Betty. We had a Flintstone theme.

The resulting record was *Shoulder to Shoulder* with the addition of Kenny Williams on keys and vocals. The songs were mostly upbeat, reflecting the band's mood. *Voice of the Spirit* was the album video. "Shoulder to Shoulder" was the single.

ALLIES signed with a Nashville booking agency. Now I was engineering, producing, and writing. Adding all of that to the touring band, it was a lot. My philosophy at the time was "wear a lot of hats; always have plenty of work." If I had it to do all over again, I wouldn't have the energy.

Bob needed zero psychology when doing vocals. His mood never affected his ability to deliver a song. Since we were co-producing records, I would ask him how he felt about something he had just sung. In one session, he cut me short and said, "Don't ask me anymore. Just call it."

From then on, I acted like an umpire (or an emperor) as I ran the tape machine. I might say, "I'm keeping the third line. Do the rest again." And Bob would just concentrate on singing. No more discussions. We worked fast.

By the fourth ALLIES record, something clicked into place. I could write part of a song and Bob could finish it. Bob could just write a verse, and I'd have the chorus. We could splice together unrelated pieces of music and still have a good song. So we got crazy. We wrote things that mixed up R&B with blues and rock. None of it fit with what Christian radio was doing at the time. This was either to be something big or a big flop.

It turned out to be something big. *Long Way from Paradise* sold like cowboy hats in Texas. It had multiple number-one singles. We had a prestigious Exit/In appearance in Nashville during Gospel Music Week. Randy Lee was with us on keys. Generally, Gospel music was ashamed of rock 'n' roll bands. But when ALLIES took the stage, we won over 500 new fans. The normally jaded Nashville crowd loved our bruiser songs that didn't conform to Christian radio!

"Crying in the Chapel" was our only cover song. The video is practically a Bob Carlisle solo appearance. (This would have been a smarter move two years later.) The man who wrote the song in 1953 was Artie Glenn. Elvis and over fifty other artists recorded the song. Artie came to a show in Dallas (home of the Bronco Bowl).

"Did you like our version of 'Cryin' in the Chapel'?"

"Like it? It knocked my hat in the crick! Love it!"

"What do you do now, Artie?"

"I do two things: Golf. And fish."

"Devil Is a Liar" and "Take Me Back" went to number one. Then Bob and I also had the Dolly Parton hit! It was our year. *Long Way from Paradise* did so well that we did what many artists do when they hit on a winning formula: We screwed it up. We did a self-indulgent record called *The River*.

The label screwed up, too. The cover looked like a red paper bag. (What's that got to do with a river?) Bob did some stellar vocals. Eat your heart out, Sammy Hagar. I like the guitar solo on "Mule Headed Man." The title song was ten minutes long! Creative oversight is a valuable thing (and we didn't have any).

Oh, well. We had a number-one country song. Our label was in Nashville. Our agency was in Nashville. And while southern California began to decline, Nashville began to beckon.

Songstory Writer Tip: If you can, write for a project with a deadline. Pro songwriters come up with the songs they need for a purpose. That may sound foreign to you. If I had to write a song with no schedule in mind, I probably wouldn't come up with a song. Last year I had lunch with Cliff Williams of AC/DC. Very nice Englishman. He mentioned that the band would be recording soon. Knowing that there was one chance in a trillion, I wrote a song. My son Randall sang it. (Well, he screamed it very musically!) It was quick. I had a deadline and a purpose. You've never heard it, because AC/DC writes its own material.

Even though I failed at a long shot, at least I gave it a shot.

Songstory XV

Of All the Places I've Ever Been and Not Know Where I Was (This Is the Place I've Been and Not Know Where I Was the Most)

I could write a million songs about the things I've done—
But I could never sing them so they'd never get sung—
There's a law for the rich and one for the poor
and there's another one for singers:
It's "Die young; live much longer; spend your money
and sit and wonder."
(From "No One Came" by Deep Purple)

We rocked the soccer-mom rental van!
(Songstory)

Jesus hung in our stead. That is the Gospel.
(Songstory)

LOOK AT THE title of this chapter and the quotes. There's too much tail on that kite. Now you're getting my money's worth. The title is a quote from one of my hilarious, yet verifiable road stories! Let's go back to a time

129

when men's shorts were shorter and the attention spans were longer....

Lost in Australia

There was a time when the British sent their convicts to Australia. I can understand why. The continent seems to be farther away than is really necessary. In the late '80s, ALLIES flew out of LAX on a Tuesday. The flight lasted twenty-four hours and we got there on a Thursday. What happened to Wednesday? The earth spun one way while we flew the other. We skipped a whole day. Seems logical that on the return flight, we'd get home before we left.

Didn't happen. Everyone on that plane should get a bonus day added on to the end of their life. Anyway...

On a rare day off, Matt, Jimmy, and I got lost in the outback going to the beach. We found the water, but where were we? The local Aussies couldn't tell us where we were, because they too were lost! We tiptoed out among the waves like Peter walking on water. There were flat rocks situated so that we could stroll ankle deep out to sea for what seemed like a mile.

Then we stood in the sun facing the unknown stretch of beach. Jimmy was deep in thought. I had a feeling that a quotable quote was coming. Sure enough, Jim carefully laid out one of his classic lines that is burned forever in my memory. He pursed his lips, and with squinted eyes, he said, "Of all the places I've ever been and not know where I was; this is the place I've been and not know where I was—the *most!*"

The Celebrity Tour

ALLIES rented vehicles. It was probably due to my experience with Sweet C blowing motors and transmissions.

There was a leg of one tour when we didn't need a van or a truck. We carried only luggage and guitars. We rented station wagons. We toured in two Chevrolet Celebrities. There was nothing spectacular about these cars. Yet we enjoyed traveling as happy vagabonds in such mediocre machines.

There was a windy night when we had finished playing and needed to gas up before leaving some dusty Midwestern town. After loading everybody up, I yelled out, "Head 'em up! Move 'em out!" (a quote from the *Rawhide* TV show theme which, of course, is owned by Universal, who owns my songs ... OK, enough Attention Surplus Detail).

As the underpowered Celebrity pulled away slowly, some ALLIES fans spotted us in a station wagon that their moms would not be caught dead in. One ran up to the rolling Chevy, peering into our dirty get-away wagon. He must have been a fan, because he pointed and yelled to his friends, "HOLY $H*T! It's ALLIES!"

Matthew waved. After the laughter died down, we knew we had our secret motto for the Celebrity Tour.

Randy Lee suggested, "Maybe that should be the title of the *last* ALLIES record!"

Roommates

Bob and I both claimed we had the best traveling roommate. Bob said, "I get in the room, and Jim drops right off to sleep. Then I have the room to myself."

I countered with, "I like Fred. He's quiet. He drops right off to sleep, too."

Fred, who rarely spoke, opined, "Then, why don't you just put us in a room together, and you won't have to pay for it!"

OOF!

ALLIES played a huge Baptist church facility. The venue was so big that Jimmy and I got lost trying to find the platform. We heard the band start without us. We panicked. We followed the sound. I headed to the right, saying, "I think it's this way!"

Jim heard a stronger sound coming from the left. He yelled out, "I think it's this way!" I zigged while Jimmy zagged.

It turned out I was right. The door I picked led to the stage area. Just then, I heard a loud "OOOF!" to my left. The "OOOF" carried with it a strange acoustic reverberation.

Jimmy had fallen into the empty baptistry.

An Ya Go An Ya Go An Ya Go
(Said Quickly with a Canadian Long Ooh Sound)

By the early '90s, Brian Fullen became my primary touring buddy. Often Bob would take a luxury rental car full of guys careening off on their own tour route. Brian and I would take the van full of gear and tootle from one Cracker Barrel to the next. I can't understand why musicians prefer tour buses and airlines. We rocked the soccer mom rental van!

Travelers now can't imagine not having a map on their phone. They also can't imagine how squirrelly directions could be in the olden days. We heard everything from "You definitely gotta leave from somewhere's else" (a twist on the old "You cain't git there from here") to "Take the underpass under the overpass and then the overpass over the underpass." But one Canadian store clerk took the proverbial cake. Brian and I asked the Canadian for directions to a local college. I'll never forget his answer:

OK, eh! Ya goooo to this *ferst* stop an goooo
light, eh? (Pause)
And then ya go. (Pause)
And then ya goooo to tha *next* stop an goooo
light eh? (Pause)
And then ya go. (Looks up at the ceiling)
And then ya goooo to tha *next* stop an goooo
light eh?
(Squints)
And then ya go. (Closes his eyes)

And then ya goooo to tha *next* stop an goooo
light eh?
And then ya go. (Long pause)
And then ya goooo to tha next stop an goooo
light eh?
(Gets an excited look)
And then....................
YA-GO-AN-YA-GO-AN-YA-GO!
(Makes a karate-chop motion with his hand)
Soooo then it's like right on yer left, there, eh? Ya
can't miss it!

And down the road, eh, there it was.
Right. On our left.

Puns with Pat Boone

ALLIES did radio and TV shows with Pat Boone. Pat
asked, "Randy, weren't you in Sweet Comfort? They were
a seminal Christian rock band!"

I said, "No, we weren't Seminoles. We were part of a
tribe called Calvary Chapel."

Then Pat introduced our ALLIES *Surrender* war
video, saying, "Let's join the fray!"

We asked, "Fray?"

Pat answered, "'Fraid so."

Steve and Marijean Green Are Too Nice

Christian artist Steve Green is kind of the opposite of me: sensible, humble, non-rock 'n' roll. He's like Pat Boone. Too straight. Lori and I loved the Greens, but, darn it, they're just too nice.

Lori and I went with Franklin Classical School for a summer retreat. Steve and Marijean Green were part of our troupe. Steve and I went out in a canoe one afternoon. We had a normal conversation. As we came in to shore, I couldn't wait to tell Lori, "I talked with Steve—and it was normal! He wasn't too nice!"

Steve and I pulled up to shore. Marijean and Lori were waiting. We pulled the canoes up on the shore like normal people. Steve and Marijean said goodbye and began walking back to camp, like normal people.

Lori whispered, "Did you guys have a good talk?"

I said, "You know, it was great. We didn't talk business, we just hung out..."

Then, up the hill ahead of us, Steve and Marijean did something that ruined everything: They began picking up trash as they walked back to camp.

I hung my head and admitted, "They did it again."

Lori agreed. "Yep. They are just too nice."

Deflated, Lori and I followed the Greens back to camp. We didn't pick up any trash, because the Greens were carrying it all. And we're not as nice as they are.

Songstory Writer Tip: Humor seems to be losing its place in current songwriting. When I was a kid, there was a comedy section in record stores. Homer and Jethro made a career out of lampooning songs. Roger Miller made a career out of it. Victor Borge discovered that people were more entertained when he introduced a song than when he played it.

Weird Al Yankovic had a long run of parodies. And he's worth $20 million if you believe everything you read. All that to say, if you can't make a career out of it, you can write at least one joke song. For the fun of it. You will thank me for the suggestion. Why? Your joke song (if it is at all funny) will be the hit of your songwriter showcases! It will make people like you.

Bob and I wrote "I'm Tired" as a joke. Of course, having Hall of Famer Hank Williams Jr. record your song is no joke. The song gets a lot of laughs at Hank's shows.

Heck, my next door neighbor has a joke song. All the locals love it! OK, put the book down and go write something funny. The next chapter will still be here when you get back.

Songstory XVI

You Ain't from Around Here, Dontcha?

When I was a kid my parents moved a lot,
but I always found them.
(Rodney Dangerfield)

GOD USUALLY DOESN'T lead people by the seat
of their pants. It's easier to steer a car that is in motion.
And God can lead you while making you think it's *your*
idea. Well, Lori and Jacque got the idea that Franklin,
Tennessee, was THE place we needed to be. Me? I had
never thought of leaving southern California. Things
change when wives pray.

While on tour in 1989, Bob and I peeled off from the
band and drove south toward Franklin. Heading down
I65 at about four in the morning, I saw a sign that said,
"Franklin, next exit." Half asleep, I slammed on the
brakes and swerved off the interstate.

There was nothing there. I rubbed my eyes. "There's
nothing here!"

Bob woke up and looked at a map. "There's nothing
here, because this is Franklin, Kentucky."

"Oh."

In a matter of hours, the sun came up while we
arrived in Franklin, Tennessee. There was something

there, just not much. There was a Holiday Inn and McDonald's. Bob called a real estate agent and went house hunting. I followed the signs that said "Hwy 96 Downtown Franklin." After a few minutes, I was lost out in the country again. I turned around. The sign said "Hwy 96 Downtown Franklin" ahead.

I finally found a town square with a Confederate soldier statue. I asked a man at a gas station where I could find a real estate agency. He squinted at me and croaked, "You ain't from around here, dontcha?"

I didn't know whether to answer "Yes, I'm not" or "No, I are."

I'm a little slow at spying out the land. Not Bob. On the drive home, Bob announced that he had purchased a house.

"What? Did you call Jacque?"

"Not yet. She'll love it. It has a barn. Plus, Jeannie C. Reilly's parents live next door!"

That was that. The Carlisles moved to 1107 Warrior Drive. It was a stone's throw from the interstate. Lori and I operated under the quant idea that both of us should *see* a home before we buy it. We flew out from California and looked through dozens of Williamson County homes. All this was for naught.

On our second trip, we arrived at the Carlisle home at midnight. Jacque ran out in her jammies. She jumped into our car. "I'm gonna show you your house!" Jacque had us drive around the corner. "There's your house!" Jacque announced. It looked like a gingerbread house high up on a rolling hill. We drove up and surveyed the home in the dark. We found a back door open. Yes. We did an illegal midnight tour of the house!

Lori said, "We can't afford this!" Turns out, Bausch and Lomb owned the house. They were anxious to unload it.

So Jacque was right. We bought it. 2483 Goose Creek By-pass was our home for the next eighteen years!

Moving to Tennessee left Jimmy, Matt, and keyboardist Randy Lee behind. We tried being a California/Nashville band for a while, but it didn't make sense. We would need a Nashville lineup. (Ironic, in that, as I write this, Matt and Jim live in the area, while Bob and I have departed.)

Even the best Nashville drummers couldn't replicate anything close to what Jim Erickson laid down. But Brian Fullen found me. He had a master's degree in music, but it didn't hurt his playing. Brian and I would go on to record thousands of songs together.

I got a call soon after. A slightly twangy voice said, "I hear you're looking for a bass player?"

"Yeah..."

"Well, I'm your guy!" Hm. Whoever this guy was, he had no shortage of confidence!

I met Mark Hill at his small apartment near the airport. The plan was to hear him play. The problem was he couldn't make any noise. It might disturb the neighbors who demanded quiet while multiple Boeing 747s passed overhead. Mark clamped earphones on my head and started to play along with one of the songs on a CD.

Even with these limitations, it took about four bars before I tapped Mark on the shoulder. "I've heard enough."

He still had headphones on. "WHAT?"

"You're in." He was that good.

About a week later, I was onstage telling an audience, "I'd like to introduce the band right now. Mark Hill, this is Bob Carlisle. Bob … Mark." They shook hands. It was the first time they had met!

Scott Sheriff was playing keys for a Christian publishing office in Nashville. We were able to sit down and run through songs. Scott joined the band. All three of these guys were my first picks, and they all worked out great. Brian went on to play with Shania Twain and countless others. Mark Hill would join Keith Urban and countless others. Scott Sheriff is playing with Carrie Underwood and has performed with countless others. Whoever "countless others" are today, they're lucky to have those boys.

In reality, God picked these guys. Just like the first bunch.

My recording gear was temporarily situated in a tiny room off of the garage. Jonathan David Brown (he from the first Sweet C record and the trombone solo) started using my recording gear on a Greg X Volz project. We traded studio time for a piano. Jonathan started saying strange things. He was hanging around skinheads in his spare time. I asked him if he was a white supremacist. He denied it by using the "n" word: "I don't hate n——s, if that's what you mean!" Oh, man.

Jonathan didn't show up one day. He was on the six o'clock news, though. *Christian music producer arrested for harboring a fugitive wanted in synagogue shooting.* We sold the piano. Lori and I wondered if the FBI was watching our house. If they did, they never came asking questions. Whew.

A studio needed to be built. Sam Scott to the rescue. The barn became a thousand-square-foot recording space. I was collecting radios. Highway 101 band recorded a song there called "Radio Ranch." Since the studio was becoming more commercial, and not just an ALLIES place, we christened it Radio Ranch. (Bob called our forested hilltop haven "Big Rock Randy Mountain"!)

Radio Ranch became the creative space for thousands of songs and recordings. Everyone from Newsboys to Stryper was a client. There were plenty of outside projects and plenty of laughs. For instance:

Keyboardist: "Get your big butt out of the way" (taking over the mike).
Bassist: "I don't think I have a big butt!"
Keyboardist: "You don't think so? Have you ever walked *behind* you before?"

The final ALLIES record was *Man with a Mission.* The band traveled the U.S. and Europe and had great fun. The dynamics were different, though. It was no longer California cronies. Bob and I were old dogs. The Nashville guys were pups.

It always felt strange changing band members. It's like substituting a family member and hoping no one notices. No two musicians play alike. But the further you go in the music business, the more you see personnel changes. Maybe it's like that in every business. But musicians are weirder than average.

Mission certainly didn't suffer from being a "Nashville" record. Why was it the last record? Because Bob had his eye on starting a solo career. It's pretty common and fairly inevitable. Why tour with a five-piece band if you can be a solo act? In Christian music, the bands starve. Solo acts play with tracks and keep the band money.

There was no Farewell Tour. No beating of the deceased equine. Bob had a clever transitional idea. We played "unplugged" dates, just Bob and me. Playing unplugged was very fashionable at that moment. Really, we still played our electric guitars. Loudly. To tracks. Unplugged? We merely unplugged from the band! It wasn't too bad. The pups continued their illustrious careers. Stick a fork in it. ALLIES was done.

This left Randy and Lori at a familiar place: starting over.

Songstory Writer Tip: Have you ever repeated a joke that nobody got? Probably not. Yet amateur songwriters will write songs that no one but the writer "gets." Then they play them over and over. As if that will help.

What good is that? The key is to *connect*. Write songs that bring the nod. The nod means "I get it. Me, too." This is why so many lyrics are somewhat vague. People like songs such as "You Got A Friend" or "Comfortably Numb." They aren't likely to nod along to "Mary Is the Girl I Shouldn't Have Married." Too specific. The aim is to write a song that all listeners can claim as their own. Go for the nod.

Songstory XVII

All Hail the Exploding Batman Pants

He didn't really like travel, of course.
He liked the idea of travel, and the memory of travel,
but not travel itself.
(Julian Barnes)

MY WIFE LORI is amazed by my attention span. She once said, "I'm glad you're not OC/DC."

My brow furrowed. "I think OC/DC is a band from Oh-stralia, darling. You mean Attention Deficit Disorder. The acronym is A.D.D."

She insisted, "Well, you have whatever is the opposite of that: You can pay attention to one detail *all day long!*" Lori has diagnosed me with Attention Surplus Syndrome.

I'm not really comfortable with the acronym.

Let's turn my attention to some more travel memories. Cut and fade to 1988. ALLIES played at Calvary Chapel in Costa Mesa with surfer dude Randy Zigler hosting. By the '80s, there were thousands of kids coming, and they heard us on Christian radio stations including KYMS. Costa Mesa: Jesus Freak Mecca! This was where the famous pants-ripping episode unfolded.

ALLIES had scoured army surplus stores for clothing and machine-gun netting that covered the equipment. Bob found an officer's uniform somewhere. Perhaps it was already somewhat well-worn. In the midst of an Elvis move that involved a spreading of the legs, Bob's military pants parted like the Green Sea! Yea, verily, what was formerly one became *two!* Drummer Jimmy had the best seat in the house to enjoy the view. "It was like *The Incredible Hulk* in reverse, man. Like Poppin' Fresh dough exploding through green rags!"

Jimmy went slant-eyed and toppled with laughter! Bob disappeared from the stage. I had never heard the band fall apart like this. Backstage, Bob commandeered a too-short pair of grey corduroy bell-bottoms. (Bell-bottoms were not quite the style anymore by the mid-'80s.) Bob finished the gig in an olive drab shirt with the non-matching grey "high-waters."

Bob's version lives on via the internet. I checked with Jim. Jimmy said, "I was in the cat-bird's seat, man. I'm the one what *knows* how it went *down!*"

The Kid on the Plane

Timing is everything. We had one flight where a five-year-old kid was repeating the entire script of the 1989 movie *Batman* with Jack Nicholson as the Joker. The boy must have been allowed to watch it a hundred times. He would erupt with Joker lines like *"Wait'll they get a load of me!"* *"You ever dance with the devil in the pale moonlight?"* *"Where does he get all those wonderful toys?"* *"We*

have a flying mouse to kill, and I wanna clean my claws!"
This went on for ninety minutes.

The kid was on everyone's last neuron. Until the crowning moment—the accidental payoff. The plane landed. The pilot announced, "Welcome to San Antonio."

The boy yelped, "THIS TOWN NEEDS AN ENEMA!"

All Hail the Power of Bob Talking

On one of the last ALLIES dates, we had an audience that was wrapped around our palm. Or perhaps they were eating out of our finger. Anyway, Bob began to wax eloquent. He was making an effort to explain the majesty of God. Waving his hand, he said, "God is the master of time and space and dimension (something in his mind started reaching for hymn lyrics) ... and *angel's prostates fall!*"

I fell over with a thump. Bob ad-libbed, "Which probably sounds a lot like THAT..." I laughed so hard, some tears ran down my leg.

As we limped through the next song, Bob whispered, "I'm gonna get in trouble for that one..."

Sure enough, afterward a little old lady wagged a boney finger at Bob saying, "I didn't appreciate what you said!" Which proves that some people have no sense of humor.

"Angel's prostates...." Just typing that still makes coffee come out of my nose.

Songstory Writer Tip: Never go on stage in vintage pants.

Songstory XVIII

The Volume of These People!
(Touring Europe)

Kilometers are shorter than miles.
Save gas; take your next trip in kilometers.
(George Carlin)

STRETCH YOUR ARMS and yawn. Stop staring at that last sentence and just do it. There. Now we're ready to continue with yet more travel stories!

Touring in Europe became a summer tradition. Holly Beyouski at Street Level Artists was booking us, and Ray wanted to keep us on the international scene. We would usually land in the enchanting land of Amsterdam.

On a few of these trips, we used Willem Van Der Poll on keyboards. I asked about his name. Willem explained, "The name Willem [pronounced Villem] is like your English name William, and Van Der Poll translates to 'of the Voting Booth.'"

I smiled. "I'll just call you Ballot Box Billy!" Villem didn't smile.

On these European jogs, we would be paired with other acts such as Larry Norman, Edwin Hawkins, Koinonia, Stryper, White Cross, and others. One trip featured Bryan Duncan with my dear buddy Steve Latanation on drums!

We spent a lot of time in Germany. In some parts of Europe, they will throw money at you if they like you. They don't throw paper currency. No. They throw coins! Ouch. I have dented guitars.

Do You Speak English?

ALLIES made an unscheduled trip to Brussels. We had no concert dates. We knew nothing of the country. We heard that our San Bernardino pastor, Dr. Don Baldwin, was headed to a Bible Institute there. We simply took a train there, thinking we'd figure things out as we went. When it came to wandering, Matthew was fearless. It was our core of Jimmy, Matt, Bob, and me. Following Matt, we got off at a train station in Brussels.

It was a warm summer day with a light breeze. I remember lots of flower boxes and chirping birds. With luggage in hand, we began wandering down a curved lane. There were quaint little abodes with stone walk-ways. We were not in the big city anymore. Little old ladies were watering flowers in front of their homes. None of them could (or would) speak English to us. We looked as out of place as we truly were. Ball caps, guitars, and cowboy boots. There was no metropolis in sight.

The cuteness wore off. We were hot and hungry. I decided that we must throw ourselves on the mercy of some French-speaking resident. Perhaps if we said "Bible Institute" and "Brussels" often enough (and loudly enough), someone would point us in the right direction. The squeaky wheel breeds contempt, right?

Matt and I walked up to one of a row of adorable country cottages. After I knocked, a lady hesitantly answered. We looked obviously American. "Bon jour," I said. That was the extent of my French. In slow and deliberate English, I said, "We are looking for the Brussels Bible Institute. Do you speak English?"

After a long pause, the most astounding thing happened; she answered, "Sure. Where're you guys from?" in a California accent like my own. I expected *Twilight Zone* music to play.

Thrown back on my boot heels, I said, "Um, Redlands. California."

"Oh," she said, " How cool! I'm from Yucaipa. I went to high school in Redlands." With that, she gave us directions.

We played fairly extensively in Germany. I had a guitar technician named Wolfgang. He would set up my equipment so perfectly, I called him my "Reinemachefrau" (cleaning woman). Wolfgang set up my equipment with precision. If I adjusted anything, he would measure it afterward so that everything would be perfect at the next gig.

There is a European tradition to do something special on the last date of a tour. On that last date, Wolfgang had my guitar carefully (temporarily) re-labeled *"Reinemachefrau"*! During the last song, what looked to be an old woman in a shawl came out and began mopping the floor in front of the band. It was Wolfgang in drag!

The German word for travel is fahrt. Now that's just asking for it! Every off-ramp invites you to ausfahrt (outfahrt). On every fahrt (trip) through the country, you are encouraged to fahrt multiple times. Before this, you make your fahrtplan; make sure you stop and eat more schnitzel! When you make an unscheduled trip, this is an extrafahrt. These are those surprise fahrts that are uncalled for.

Being of partial German heritage, I liked to flatter myself that I could speak a little of the language. Bob would tell me that I was rattling on in fluent German in my sleep. Bob tried to stop a sleep-speech I was giving one German evening. He said I sat up and yelled, "You're too *fat!*"

He said, "I know. Go back to sleep."

Later, other band members said that while in Germany, I spoke only German in my sleep. (Can't imagine what I'd have to say.)

We had a very different experience in Scandinavia. We would often go to Kragero, Norway, outside of Oslo, to play for a festival I cannot pronounce: Skarsgardsgospel. The promoter was called Morton Strand. We asked him for his real name, but he firmly refused, saying, "You could not pronounce it." We were offended. The first night of these events would begin with a dinner. Each artist was seated at a table of Norwegians, Swedes, and Finns.

I would say, "My name is Randy."

The other guests would say:

"My name is Fyyorrkpt."

"My name is Yerelghphlemnscrrp."

"Ya, and I am Ooogrnsorskensensonsoonsonsen."

These were all names I could not pronounce, let alone remember!

"May I just call you all 'Vortex'? Twos in Tock!"

Genesis teaches that God confused our language. I'm certainly confused. The Germans speak Deutsche. Nederlanders speak Dutch. In Belgium they speak Belch. And the French are learning Aramaic.

In Scandinavia, I became perplexed with the ubiquitous term "vaer sa god" (this sounds like "vahshagoo"). They will tell you this means "Here you are," but of course they are lying. I heard "vahshagoo" when the meaning taken was "You're in my way" or "You're holding up the line" or "I'm glad that Jimmy just handed me all of his money and is trusting me to give him the correct change."

I've decided that *vaer sa god* means "*Stupid American.*"

The Volume of These Americans

Walking the streets of Amsterdam is great fun, although you need to be aware of your surroundings.

Our crew had been loading equipment into a church when some local pitched in to help. He helped himself to my guitar. We assumed he was a drug addict. A church janitor decided to check the recessed doorways down the street. He found the thief with my guitar pressed to his chest. The janitor retrieved my instrument and explained to the would-be thief in Dutch that "stealing was not nice."

On the occasions when the band roamed the city, we would often be clopping down cobbled streets in cowboy boots, laughing loudly. We must have echoed down the lane.

An older gentleman scuffled along a sidewalk while we strode down the street like a platoon. In curmudgeonly fashion, he grumbled something to himself in Dutch. I asked Villem, "What did he say?"

Villem gave me the quick transliteration. "He said, 'The *volume* of these people!'" The Volume of These People became the title of that tour!

All Dressed Up, Nowhere to Rock

ALLIES also did a "White Metal Tour" of Europe with Stryper and Whitecross. (White *metal*? Whatever.) On one date in Germany, we got all three bands on the bus, ready to go to the hall for the "big show" that evening. Every American head of hair was sprayed as high as possible. The ALLIES guys were slightly dressed up and cologned. The Whitecross guys were more outfitted and head-banded. The Stryper guys were in sexy yellow-and-black-striped spandex with full lipstick and stunning makeup!

The bus pulled out. The tour manager made a phone call to the hall. I caught the gist of the conversation in German: The gig was canceled. The bus made three quick right metropolitan turns and brought us right back to the hotel entrance within funf Deutsch minuten.

While the other bands went back to remove costumes and eyeliner, we ALLIES guys walked right into a restaurant to enjoy a rare night off from white metal.

Know Any Twirls?

Stryper drummer Robert was a friendly guy. His hair and teeth were so pretty. When he had his makeup and spandex on, Bob would say admiringly, "I'd go bowlin' with him." We watched many Stryper shows where Robert would pound the drums and do tricks. He would showboat and throw sticks in the air; take his hat off, put it back on; all while playing. He did this at the expense of the groove. You could see the other band members scrambling to recover the beat.

ALLIES drummer Brian is precise and dependable. Dead on. Brian also was highly trained, educated, and wrote books on the art of drumming. I knew the day was coming.

Backstage, Brian was practicing rudiments on a road case. Swiss triplets, ratamacues, and triple paradiddles. All with impressive precision. Robert sat down across from Brian and enthused, "Dude! Do you like, know any twirls?"

There was a pause while Brian processed the question. He had studied extensively without learning any show-stopping (and groove-killing) tricks. It had never occurred to him. Brian smiled apologetically at Robert and pretty much ended the conversation in one syllable:

"No...."

The Mystery Fountain

Bob and I shared a Swiss hotel room with a mysterious fountain fixture in it. We were fascinated with it. We puzzled over its necessity, since we also had a bathtub, sink, and toilet. (Maybe this is where you go Number Three?) We enjoyed our Euro-drinking fountain. After the charm wore off, it became a urinal. The following day we were informed by our Euro-band guys that these are called a "bidet." You clean your back-side with it.

All I can say is that Swiss guys are weird.

Larry Norman and Charles Normal

Larry Norman was always an adventure. The first time I saw Larry perform, he had Kevin Thomson doing sound. While playing, Larry griped so much about the sound that Kevin quit, turned off the system, and stormed out of the auditorium.

Larry was respected as the "father of Christian rock." He was so enigmatic that I found it disappointing to see him in concert. Sorry. (I'll get hate mail for this.) I just didn't think his singing was that impressive. Nice hair, though.

We did some European media interviews with Larry and other artists. This is where I learned what all the hoopla was about: Larry could be in a room with thirty other artists and become the undisputed star of the show.

In Sweden, we met a Finnish band called Q-Stone. I thought they were amazing. (Finns playing electric blues?) Q-stone told us about touring with Larry. They saw two sets of microphones being placed on the equipment at a festival. They asked Larry, "Are you recording this show?" Larry assured them he wasn't. Norman released the live record soon afterward. While the band didn't mind doing it for free, they thought it was kind of weird.

One afternoon, Lori and I were trapped by a Dutch rain storm in a small cabin with Larry and his brother Charles, who used the last name Normal. It was the early '90s. Sitting for an hour with Larry talking was not boring. Lori asked, "Where are you guys staying?"

"Oh, we're just camping out in a field."

"In a cabin, like this?"

"No, just a tent." Every time Larry said something, Charles Normal nodded.

Larry began to tell us about the KGB trying to kill him in 1988. I was skeptical. "Really? The KGB?"

Mr. Norman and Mr. Normal nodded. "Someone had slipped something into my food," Larry said. "I must have passed out, and I woke up in a hospital. I had a blue gown on and tubes were in my veins. I heard the nurses talking with men in the hallway, and I got the idea that they were either going to kill me or put me in an asylum. I climbed out of a window and escaped. Then I had to escape the country, without the KGB arresting me!" Charles remained mute and nodded.

Lori and I were a little confused. "Larry, why do you think you were such a threat to the Soviet Union?"

"I don't know."

"While you were incapacitated, I'm surprised that the KGB didn't take your passport and clothing."

"Yeah. It was weird." Charles looked perturbed and said nothing. When someone came to pick up Lori and me, we said goodbye to Mr. Norman and Mr. Normal.

Lori and I rode in silence for a while. I had a witness to what I had witnessed. I asked Lori, "So, what did you think of Larry Norman and Charles Normal?"

She said, "I don't think either one of them was normal..."

Hi, Kitty! Hi, Kitty!

Pope John Paul II was visiting his home country of Poland. This was a big deal. (Popes are supposed to be from Italy.) We had never opened for a pope before. Band manager Ray Ware came with us. We made our way toward Poland by aged passenger trains. The landscape was getting more barren and grey by the mile. We had been somewhat coddled in Western Europe, where most people are capitalistic enough to speak English.

There was a train station where we were to board a Polish train going through Czechoslovakia. The place smelled like an outhouse at low tide. Bob pointed out an ominous logo on some of the cars—they were still stamped with the hammer and sickle of the former USSR. It gave us chills.

Boarding a Czech train with six scruffy Nashville musicians and thousands of pounds of gear did not work well. Ray stopped the rickety train while Brian and I brought up the rear with a large cart of equipment. We shoved the stuff onto the decrepit passenger car, into compartments and hallways.

The conductors took our passports. They literally hid them and refused to give them back. Since we didn't know the language, a more universal language was used: U.S. dollars. We had to bribe whoever these guys were. It was a tiny international episode that ended with all the people on the train hating us. We didn't blame them. So we blamed Ray. Disgusted, the group informed Ray Ware that he was the worst road manager *ever*.

The disgusted pups (younger band members) settled down in one compartment. Bob and I (the disgusted old dogs) plopped in another. Ray was banished. Banished to his own dingy compartment. As Bob and I sat across from each other, the ancient train began to resume the departure. It moved at a turtle's pace, leaving a grey old station in the grey old Czech town.

In the compartment next to us, we heard Ray lower his window. A skeletal feline was walking the adjacent rails. She was walking faster than the train was moving.

Ray cried out, "Hi kitty! Hi kitty!"

Bob and I locked eyeballs. Ray has lost it. Snapped. I can't really capture the pitiful humor in this moment.

Ray was reaching out for a friend.

Our destination was Czestochowa (pronounced "Chesta-HOVE-uh" with phlegm in the "hove"). It was an amazing sight. Tens of thousands of Catholics made their pilgrimage from around eastern Europe to get a peek at the pope. Money changers were everywhere. Still embedded in my mind is the body language of the Catholics there. They bowed. They lay prostrate. (Not to be mistaken with prostate.)

There was an eerie combination of holiness and desperation. The Scripture says much about humility. I was imagining the Lord attending closely to these anguished prayers. Who cares about religion or language?

Musicians from the West had been invited into "Polska." Before the pope's visit, this had not been allowed. We were part of a huge music celebration, culminating in a papal appearance. That's why I say, "We opened for the pope."

We shared a stage with Donna Summers, Leon Patillo, BeBe and CeCe Winans, and the fabulous Shirley Caesar. Shirley gets her own adjective because she deserves some kind of a storm warning. Our band at that time was powerful, passionate, and *loud*. But I felt that Shirley outdid us like a Cat-5 hurricane compared to a thunderstorm.

We became Shirley Caesar fans right there. And Shirley is making Jesus fans.

Songstory Writer Tip: Change venues. If you always write in your office, it can be stifling. Touring musicians benefit from the changing scenery. Traveling always helped me stay creative. Guitarists have the advantage here. Go out into the woods. A front porch can give you a view of the world. Stare at a screensaver of Ireland or some land you've never been to. I hear the Eiffel Tower has a lot of songs in it! Changing venues will help get some variety in your songs. If not, at least you'll get out once in a while.

I do not recommend writer's rooms in Nashville. People write hit songs in spite of them, not because of them.

Songstory XIX

Jesus Christ: He's Strong;
Weak in No Way
(PolyGram Daze)

Music is spiritual. The music business is not.
(Van Morrison)

Sing to the Lord a new song.
(Psalm 5; Psalm 15; Psalm 33; Psalm 40; Psalm 95;
Psalm 96; Psalm 98; Psalm 144; Isaiah 42)

MUSIC ROW WAS busier than a one-legged termite in
a dead oak tree in the mid-'90s. Bob launched his solo
career with Sparrow Records. After a year of chasing the
Big Country Deal with Sony, I prayed for some steady
employment. I also needed to widen my songwriter asso-
ciations. Manager David Smallbone introduced me to
Gordon Kennedy. In his charming Australian accent,
David referred to Gordon as a "class act." ("Class" rhymes
with "gloss" when David says it.)

Gordon's dad is Jerry Kennedy, a highly accomplished
producer who played the guitar part on Roy Orbison's
"Pretty Woman." Gordon had been in the Christian band
Whiteheart. His songwriting and playing are top tier.

Gordon's recommendation to Doug Howard at
PolyGram fast-tracked a deal. Doug has an easily

imitated southern whine when he talks. Doug's lieutenant at the time was Daniel Hill. Daniel's wife was PolyGram's receptionist; let's say her name was Hope. Daniel's buddy and professional manager (song plugger) was Billy Lynn. These two were such good buddies that they were referred to as Daniel "HillBilly" Lynn!

I signed a three-year contract. PolyGram was a big player. I switched from writing just with Bob to writing with a dozen or more new acquaintances. We gathered in cubicles in those Nashville high-rises and cranked out song after song after song.

Gordon played me "Change the World," a song that had been hanging around for years. The demo sounded very Beatle-esque. It was haunting. Wynonna cut it, but Clapton made it into a monster hit.

When accepting the Grammy, Gordon said (skipping over the words "I'd like to thank"), "My Savior and Lord, Jesus Christ. He's strong; weak in no way." He then went on to thank others.

Whoa. That to me is truly "praising the Lord."

After Gordon and I had filed away some cool songs, I got a call from someone in Europe. Englebert Humperdinck had recorded a Kennedy/Thomas song, "The Great Divide."* I called Gordon.

"Hey! Good news! Englebert Humperdinck recorded one of our songs!"

(Pause)

---

* Internet footnote: Hugh Williams and Gordon Kennedy are credited on the album as writing the song. Odd. I don't even know Hugh Williams.

"What's the *good* news?"

Bob McDill was one of PolyGram's most successful writers at the time. I would see him with worn boots up on a desk, sitting alone with a yellow legal pad. Sometimes I would say, "Hi Bob! How's it going?"

He'd usually answer, "Oh, pretty good. I wrote two lines today." Bob clocked in and wrote about eight hours a day. He was also the office grump.

One day Ol' McDill quit. Some corporate shift had disgusted him. He packed a box of stuff from his desk and walked out. The receptionist said, "You can't just quit, Bob. What are you going to do with all those songs running around in your head?"

Bob snapped back, "There won't be any songs runnin' around in my head!" And, just like that, he turned the song spigot off. (I've read that Bob got disgusted again and turned the spigot back on…)

Speaking of receptionists, I couldn't help but overhear arguments between Daniel Hill and his wife "Hope" Hill. She was working with Scott Hendricks on a debut record. Scott was married. I remember being invited to one of the sessions. Hope was married to Daniel. There was some naughty extracurricular activity going on between artist and producer. It was uncomfortable seeing it firsthand.

Singer Robert Streets was becoming the hairdresser to the Nashville elite. One day, he had a lady in his salon chair, and he was happily chatting. He had seen the hanky-panky, too. He was going on and on about Mrs.

Hill and Mr. Hendricks. Then he noticed that all his hair-dressers were frantically signaling him in the mirrors. They were pointing to the lady in Robert's chair. Robert said, "I'm sorry. Have I said the wrong thing?"

The woman in his chair smiled. "No. It's fine. Scott Hendricks is my husband."

The salon went silent.

She broke the silence with, "That's the most expensive girlfriend he'll ever have…"

(In Nashville, that's what we call a good line.)

Hope Hill started to hit big. When performing, there was something oddly unpredictable about Hope. Her shows were astounding in either a good way or a bad way. I traveled with fiddle player Stuart Duncan, who played in Hope's band. I asked, "Is Hope kind of inconsistent as a singer?"

Stuart said, "She's like a faucet, man."

I was confused. "What do you mean?"

He smirked. "She only runs hot or cold!"

In the supermarket, we would see tabloids and music fanzines telling glossy stories about Nashville music stars. They print about 95 percent lies. (They get 5 percent credit for spelling the names correctly.) The real Music City Babylon was a soap opera. Everybody on Music Row knew everybody else's business. They call it Little Big Town. It seems as though the Nashville publicists are the only ones who are good at keeping secrets.

God sees it all (Proverbs 15:3). Thankfully, there's plenty of mercy to go around. By God's common grace, Hope and Scott and Daniel went on to other relationships and other successes. People do change and grow. (Excepting journalists perhaps...)

God's common grace is rich. Trey Bruce told me an amazing story. (Trey's dad Ed was the legendary writer of "Mamas, Don't Let Your Babies Grow Up to Be Cowboys.") In the early '90s, Trey was writing for MCA. Since he was delivering pizzas on the side, he went to ask his publisher Al Cooley for more money. (The draw was $8,000 a year.) Not only did Al refuse, he also let Trey go. Trey was wondering, "What next? I guess I've hit bottom." Just as he was leaving the MCA office for the last time, the receptionist stopped him. Trey had a phone call.

"Hello?"

"Trey! Scott Hendricks. I want to start a new publishing company called Big Tractor. You'll be my partner and first writer. That is, if I can pry you away from MCA..."

I'm not sure if Trey believed in God. But God believed in Trey. God puts blessings in the paths of both Christians and non-Christians. These little miracles are like God's calling card. *Truly, you are a God who hides himself, O God of Israel, the Savior (Isaiah 45:15).*

Trey watched how I produced recordings in the laid-back L.A. tradition. He said, "You need to come to one of my sessions." The Nashville session clock starts at 10, 2, and 6 (almost like Dr. Pepper). Trey gathered his players and played them a song. They each made a quick "numbers" chart. Then, the musicians picked up their instruments and performed the song as if they'd known it all their lives.

I had to overhaul the way I did sessions and charts. Drummer Brian Fullen helped me. Learning how to do the Nashville number system really sped up my life. To this day, you could play me a country song or worship song, and I'll be able to chart it in one pass. I never got to be a true Nashville session guy. I didn't need to. I was a studio owner that could hire them. The bench was mighty deep with stellar players.

Being a staff writer for a major publisher is somewhat deceptive. My songs were recorded by Hank Williams Jr., Mel McDaniels, Lila McCann, Colin Raye, Bob Carlisle, and others. I knew the connection behind every cut. If I didn't have a connection, the songs didn't get cut (unless the Finger of God came down—which it sometimes did!). The common conversation at a "write" was:

"Is your publisher getting you any cuts?"
"No … is yours?"

One exception to the lazy plugger/publisher was Russ Zavitson. He took "Achy Breaky Heart" around and played it for everybody. I hated it. That didn't faze Russ.

The Oak Ridge Boys passed. He pitched it to the unknown Billy Ray Cyrus, who probably preferred his own songs. Finally it got released, and it was so irritating, it was a huge hit.

Russ told me about tracking down the writer of the song, Don Von Tress. Don was on a construction site, screwing in drywall. *Zzzzzzzt. Zzzzzzzt.*

"Hey, Don! 'Achy Breaky Heart' is going to go number one!"
"Really?" *Zzzzzt.* "That's great." *Zzzzzt.*
"Don't you want to celebrate?"
"No, thanks." *Zzzzzt.* "I gotta finish up here." *Zzzzzt.*

Apparently, Don was going to believe it when he saw it. Which, in the music business, is not a bad idea.

Here's a self-incriminating story I should not tell you: I was writing with Bob DiPiero and Rick Crawford on Music Row. Rick had an artist deal with Warner Brothers. He was in the Artist Protection Program of the label. (His recordings never got released!) Bob was on a hot streak writing multiple hits every year. Rick said something about the song "Wink." I hissed, "I hate that song."

DiPiero and Rick looked uncomfortable. I swallowed. I think what I swallowed was my foot.

DiPiero responded with, "Well, I kind of like it … every time I go to the *bank*!"

I felt like twenty-four cents short of a quarter. It was Bob's song. I had committed the sin of criticizing a hugely successful song, thinking my songs were just as good. If they were just as good, why was everybody recording

DiPiero songs? DiPiero wrote songs that artists recorded and people loved.

Being an inferior writer to DiPiero and saying that comment appeared to be petty jealousy. Even if I had more hits than Bob, saying that would make me appear as a jerk (which, at that moment, I was)! Well, quick apologies got me some cheap forgiveness. But DiPiero was cool. We wrote a song. Nothing came of it, probably because I wasn't writing simple enough and smart enough, like Bob DiPiero.

Selah.

Tom Douglas at Sony was an interesting guy to write with. He didn't fit the normal pattern. Tom would make up pieces of nonsense songs randomly. I recorded his disconnected fits and bits. When he hit on something I liked, I'd stop him.

"Let's use that!"

"I have no idea what I did." Then I would play the tape. The adventure would repeat with lyrics. He'd make up a stream of disembodied words. I would corral some of them to keep. Somehow, we wrote a song called "I Wish I Could." The Sony people called it the Jar Song.

I wish I could save these moments;
and put 'em in a jar.
I wish I could stop the world from turning—
keep things just the way they are…

Colin Raye recorded it. The heads at Sony flipped. They wined and dined Lori and me. Plans were discussed about a Kodak commercial using the "save these moments" from the Jar Song. Sony geared up to throw their weight behind "I Wish I Could." Lori thought, "Finally. Something to shine the light onto something new! No more 'Butterfly Kisses' blues." We anticipated the big hit.

It never came.

Colin had done a song called "The Eleventh Commandment." It was anti-child abuse. Who could have a problem with that? There was *major* blowback. People don't like it when musicians get preachy. (I've told my congregation that a *thousand* times!)

Colin Raye seemed like a well-intentioned artist who was hoping to protect children. He pretty much got canceled for it. Peabo Bryson also did a great version of the Jar Song. Now we had a country version and an R&B version! Although it was a minor hit, I still consider it one of my best songs.** Now, let's talk about songwriter performances.

The Original Versions

Songs are what fuel Nashville. A song is being sung on every corner. Writer's nights are a major tourist attraction. For the writers, it is immediate gratification! The Bluebird Café has been made into a legendary venue.

I kind of hated playing the Bluebird. Maybe it's a treat for tourists. It was a circus trying to get in. There wasn't a stage. It was a tiny circle in the middle of the tables. After you finished a set, you suddenly became *persona non grata*. "Could you get out of the way? We got more writers comin' in." I preferred home-spun places like Woody's in Franklin, or Puckett's.

I learned to book my own writer's group under the name The Original Versions. We did corporate gigs

---

** One of my very best songs was with Reggie Hamm. We wrote "Nicole Hadley's Heart." A Cross Between recorded it. The real Nicole had been a Christian high school girl from Paducah, Kentucky, who had a premonition about her death. She asked her parents to sign an organ donor document for her—should anything happen.

Nicole was gunned down with two other students during Bible study. After her death at age fourteen, Nicole's heart was successfully transplanted, saving a man's life. Look her up. It will make you weep. As we wrote in the song, Nicole Hadley's heart beats on.

On the day that Nicole's song was to be released, there was a horrendous school shooting. "Nicole Hadley's Heart" was deemed insensitive. The song was pulled from radio. It would look as if we were trying to capitalize on another tragedy. I call that irony. It also leads ironically well into the next chapter.

(NOT the Bluebird). I could call the biggest writers in Nashville and get them all. I'd use only those writers who had multiple number-one hits. It's not that I had that much pull. I had something better: a budget! The conversation usually went like this:

"Hello?"
"Hey, it's Randy Thomas. Wanna do a writer's night?"
"Ugh. I don't know..."
"It's at the Ryman."
(Perks up) "Really? I've always wanted to play the Ryman..."
"It pays 500 bucks."
"I'M IN!"

One of these events was held at the Country Music Hall of Fame. Gordon was one of my Original Versions writers. There was a Garth Brooks impersonator that they hired to work the audience glad-handing. As we started playing, we could see the fake Garth Brooks with a long line of autograph seekers and photo takers. Like bees on an artificial flower.

I said (on mic) to Gordon, "Hey, Gord ... why do you suppose people are lined up to get the autograph of a Garth Brooks *impersonator*?"

Gordon speculated, "Maybe they're Garth Brooks *fan* impersonators!"

There was a joke that went around Nashville in those days: What's the difference between God and Garth Brooks?

God doesn't think *He's* Garth Brooks!

You know who first told me that joke? Garth Brooks! Maybe he started it.

Meanwhile, back at Radio Ranch: Doug Howard and Daniel Hill called a meeting with me. It was the end of my three-year deal. Doug whined, "Randy, you've been writing some great songs, buddy, but there's nothin' that's really breakin' loose for you."

I was thinking, *That's because nobody in this office ever pitches my songs!*

I raised my eyebrows. "So—are you not going to offer me another deal?"

Doug shook his head. Where was the God of the Trey Bruce miracle? Daniel looked uncomfortable. "Sorry. Gotta let you go. Numbers just don't add up."

Later that year, "Butterfly Kisses" hit. The numbers added up just fine after that. PolyGram (who had done nothing) no longer had to pay me any advances. They just raked in lots and lots of money. For advancing me a little bit of money.

And that is why they call it the music *business*.

Songstory Writer Tip: Write it bad. Fix it later.

A couple of pro Nashville writers said to me, "Let's not get bogged down. Let's get some music going. We'll just ... write it bad. Then fix it later."

The story goes that McCartney wrote a song called "Scrambled Eggs." He knew it was not the keeper lyric. He just needed placeholder words. The keeper lyrics occurred to him later ("Yesterday"). This is very common. If you relate to starting with music, just throw some nonsense lyrics in. Fix it later. I think this is how 90 percent of great songs are written.

Once my songwriting partner Bob wrote an ALLIES song called "Rock 'n' Roll Angel." He left me room to put in finished lyrics. YouTube it. Notice the lyric, "This is the place I need another line." That was Bob's placeholder! I've read that John Lennon often told McCartney to keep some of his placeholders, e.g., "The movement you need is on your shoulder." I distinctly remember telling Bob to keep it. It just sounded brilliant to me.

I guess what I'm suggesting is—fix anything that is trite, subpar, or predictable. Keep the "happy accidents"! Following this tip will keep your writing moving quickly. It should be fun! I can't stress enough—FIX IT LATER. I have written multiple choruses before picking the best one. This is what pros do.

Songstory XX

"Sometimes the Magic Works; Sometimes It Doesn't"

(Quote from 1970 movie *Little Big Man*
character Old Lodge Skins)

*I have not failed. I've just found 10,000 ways
that won't work.*
(Thomas Edison)

AFTER ALLIES, I was searching for the Next Big
Thing. Or at least "The Next Big Thing until the Next Big
Thing Comes Along," to quote Reggie Hamm. If I had it
to do over again, I might have found a singer to replace
Bob and continue with the ALLIES band. But I had the
idea that swapping singers was *not* the quality move.

Singer Robert Streets and I formed a country duo
called Alias Smith & Jones. (Which one was Smith? You
decide.) We started gathering cool songs and tried to
get that major record deal. Trey Bruce joined in. David
Smallbone and Ray Ware managed us. My ALLIES guys
Brian Fullen and Mark Hill did a lot of recording with
us. It was pretty rockin' country.

Hair-guru Robert showed up one day with red finger
tips. I asked, "What's with the red fingers?"

"Oh, that Reba's new hair color! She came in the
salon today and said, 'Robert, I want you to make me my

own color of Reba red. And I mean RED! I want people to look at my hair and say, DERN!'"

Robert hand-mixed a custom color known as DERN RED. Warning: That stuff will turn your fingers Reba red. Dern.

Big fish Sony Music Entertainment showed interest in signing Alias Smith & Jones. They asked us for a proposal. How much advance money would we need? That's a trick question, isn't it? We asked Sony for an advance beyond $100K. The negotiations cooled. Oh, well. We probably blew our chance at the Big Deal. Maybe we should have asked for just $50K...

While recording demos for Warner Brothers, Highway 101, and lots of other side projects, I befriended a Christian duo composed of Scott Riggan and Ben Bauman called the Nobodys. We did some indie projects together that served the purpose of selling some records for the boys.

Cal Turner III was the young billionaire son of Cal Turner II. Cal Turner I was CEO of Dollar General. Cal III's baby son Cal was fourth in the line of Cals, so he named his publishing concern Cal IV. Got it? I started negotiation with the new company. Cal (III) said he wanted to start a label. I pitched the Nobodys. Cal slapped his boot and said, "Let's do a record on them!"

We recorded a great record with the guys. The players on the project looked and sounded a lot like that old ALLIES band! Scott was a well-adjusted singer. He didn't need the usual studio psychology to get creative. Ben came up with an interesting take on "Eleanor Rigby."

I thought it would be a huge college hit. Their original songs would be great for Christian radio.

Cal Turner hired some new guys to run Cal IV. Can you guess who? Daniel Hill and Billy Lynn! (It's a small world. But I wouldn't want to weed-whack it.) Daniel and Billy had to figure out how to run a new company. Cal had probably been premature starting a label, you know, without an actual staff, or name, or anything. The HillBilly team shelved the record.

It was a great-sounding, well-crafted failure.

Buddy Killen was the revered publishing genius in Nashville. He had built Tree Publishing and sold it for some obscene sum. So he bought some large buildings in Nashville and started Killen Music Group. Buddy Killen had already bought and sold one of *my* music catalogs before I met him.

I would sometimes meet with Buddy in his opulent office overlooking 21st Street. He wore shark-skin suits and had a toupee that looked like a very expensive grey hat. (I kept thinking, *Don't stare at it.*) He even smelled expensive. I really liked Buddy. Everybody liked Buddy. He had come up as a bass player in the days when country music was about comedy and kitsch. His daughter and son-in-law were running a Christian label called Damascus Road. We cut a deal.

Then Buddy sold his country publishing company to Cal Turner. I felt like a guy in an earthquake movie where the ground splits underneath your feet. I was standing over the gap of a duel contract. I was writing *country* music for Cal Turner at Cal IV; I was writing

Christian music for Buddy Killen at KMG. These were the two wealthiest guys in town! My contracts were split between competitors. What could possibly go wrong?

Cal kept playing me a song called "Breathe." He said it would be a big hit. I didn't get it. Well, I was wrong. Cal IV's first big song was "Breathe" recorded by "Hope" Hill. I had heard the demo eighteen months before its release in 1997. So Daniel Hill was running Cal IV and "Hope" Hill had a hit with it. The saga continues: Both "Breathe" and "Butterfly Kisses" are now owned by Universal Music Publishing Group (UMPG, for those of you who like to try to pronounce acronyms).

These are just some of my missed guesses. I was surprised with the Dolly hit and "Butterfly Kisses." I wrote a song with Reggie Hamm called "Nicole Hadley's Heart" that is the best thing I've ever been a part of in my estimation (which failed).

Why is it that God doesn't tell us which stuff will work and which won't? Proverbs 16:9 says, "The heart of man plans his way, but the Lord establishes his steps." I believe in the sovereignty of God. I just wish He wasn't so secretive! I call Him the Keeper of Secrets.

The Lord let me move on to something else that was *great*. It just didn't succeed.

Songstory Writer Tip: Get some distance from your writing. Use your phone memo, or record some other quick way. Listen back critically the next day. Fix what bugs you. Play it for a spouse or friend. If they give you no useful advice, move on. The ones who give you useful feedback are golden.

Some writers are in a hurry to finish. They can't wait to see how it turns out! (Generally, if you write quickly, you write badly.) Think of it as a sprint and a marathon. Good songs usually start with a starter pistol bang. Then the tedium sets in. The hard part is finishing well.

Kind of like writing a book.

Songstory XXI

Identical Strangers Meets NewSong

You always pass failure on your way to success.
(Mickey Rooney)

If you think "music business" is an oxymoron,
try adding "Christian" to it!
(Randy Thomas)

ANDY DENTON IS a tall, quiet Texan with a soaring rock voice. Just like me, except for being quiet and having a soaring voice. Andy had been the singer with Ruscha and Legend Seven.

Using my legendary Attention Surplus Syndrome memory, I took the name Identical Strangers from an obscure *Mad* magazine's Snappy Answers to Stupid Questions book from the 1960s.

One page portrayed a mother with twin sons. On the next page stood a guy asking the stupid question, "Are they twins?"

To which the mother responds sarcastically, "No, they are identical strangers."

My source was so culturally random by 1996 that we didn't even research the name. The album *Identical*

Strangers was a return for me to Christian music. I was starting from scratch for a third time.

Writing for this record brought a new challenge; we had to be aware of "updating" the approach to chords and melody. Styles had shifted. We had to do the unthinkable. We had to listen to Christian radio. The gated-'verb '80s sound had been outlawed. My response was to draw on some '60s influences and fuse them with the '90s. I developed an internal dictum: Anything that sounds '80s spells death.

Our label was Buddy's Damascus Road, headed by Kent Songer. Rob Michaels was managing us. It was a whole new team. For the studio band, I called my "usual suspects" Fullen, Hill, and Brian Wooten (Wooten is now with Trace Adkins). Brian did some writing and a lot of playing on the record. Richie Biggs did tracking and mixing. I did the laborious in-between recording, known as "overdubs." By now, we were recording digitally. Digital machines made sense to me—it wasn't as big a learning curve as computers would later be! Andy sang without benefit of the tuning devices that everyone uses now (Autotune). He had to endure me working him pretty hard. I felt that the record achieved what we wanted artistically. It had its own sound.

Julianna Wilson

The first single, "Extraordinary Love," did well, and our local WayFM played it constantly. (A heavenly shout out to WayFM GM Jeff Taylor!) Then the second single,

"Julianna Wilson," got spun even more! We did a video for "Julianna Wilson" using my '64 Ford Galaxie (a rare YouTube find). Andy and I wrote the song with Wooten. I remember Brian had started with the placeholder title "Similina Pilcher," which was inspired by some John Lennon gibberish.

Brian and I made up a name out of thin air. The name Julianna flowed nicely. Wilson came from the Beach Boys' surname—just for fun. In the song, Julianna is a model with an eating disorder looking for the meaning of real beauty. She finds her inner beauty in Christ. It was fiction. Or so we thought.

Imagine our surprise when the real Juliana Wilson CALLED! I was dumbstruck. (Not a big reach for me.) Juliana said the story in the song was the story of her life. That's God Stuff, when art, ministry, and real life connect like that!

While we were downsizing to a smaller label, Bob was downsizing to a smaller label. There was a sneaking suspicion that we had stepped down from the major league to the minors. Bob called our new duo Istrangical Dentlers.

Identical Strangers toured with Atlanta-based NewSong. We were glomming onto their tour dates and doing an opening set. After twenty-five years of touring, it was nice to start again at the bottom! (This was typed with a sarcastic smirk.)

The NewSong guys were great. Leonard Ahlstrom was a prolific writer who played guitar and sang with them. He was living in Nashville and commuting often to Atlanta. Leo and I became buddies and sometimes wrote country music together.

Ice Bagger

I caught the lead singer, Russ Lee, in a gaffe one night. After a hard night of singing, playing, and signing autographs, a young girl caught him just as he was headed for the bus to collapse. She said, "I was bagging ice for the concert tonight, and ... could you sign my CD?"

Russ was so tired that "bagging ice" didn't quite compute. In his exhaustion, Russ said, "So....you're an @$$ bite? An ice bite? I mean, an ice bagger?" Poor Russ apologized profusely, but the fresh-faced fan hadn't caught the gaffe.

I did.

I heard this from around the corner. Russ didn't know I was there. Later, when he was crumpled in the tour bus, I stood over him and asked, "So ... you're an ice bite? Ice bagger?" (The NewSong guys were very sincere, good ol' Baptist non-cussers. To say the "a" word—especially to a well-meaning young fan—was highly embarrassing to Russ. This is why I simply had to exploit it.) Russ squirmed.

I made little notes for Russ—leaving them in his Bible, guitar, and on his bunk. They simply said, "Icebagger." Russ would cringe and beg me not to ever tell anyone. Russ Lee: Your secret is safe.

Security Detail

In one church they had a security detail. They dressed like FBI agents. Two on either side, with a dwarf man in the middle. Hands folded. Communication devices in one ear. I'd never seen anything like it.

While we played, the security detail stood with us onstage facing outward. In the middle was always the well-dressed tiny guy. They provided security as we loaded out afterward. The NewSong guys, Andy, and I sat mute in the bus as we pulled out.

Finally, Andy asked, "What's with the dwarf?" He was really bothered.

I asked, "Do you have a problem with 'little people'?"

The guys waited for Andy's answer. I'll never forget it. It's not PC. He said, "Well, I just wish they would stick to their own kind!"

Big, Big, Day

NewSong had a family who followed them around the South. Mom, Dad, and two boys. They would give the band gifts, such as pillows or boxes of donuts. (Unneeded, and unneeded!) They were very sweet folks. At one sound check, the dad went up to the sound guy and said, "Yep. It's a big, big, day." The sound man nodded. Then the dad went over to Russ and said, "It's a big, big, day!" Russ smiled and continued soundcheck.

Then the dad came over to me and Leo. He stood next to us, and said, "Big, big, day!"

Leo asked him, "What do you mean, 'Big, big, day'?"

The dad grinned from port to starboard—he was so glad that Leo asked! He proudly announced, "Cat had her kittens; me and the boys gots new shoes!"

Leo agreed. That is a big, big, day.*

"Butterfly Kisses" Hits

It was while Identical Strangers was on tour with NewSong that "Butterfly Kisses" hit. It was confusing. In some cities, TV stations would send a limo for me (big, big day). I was partners with Andy now. Bob was back in Nashville, with Ray Ware and a whole team managing publicity. I guess I'm not good at manipulating the media. I would tell them about writing "Butterfly Kisses." They didn't understand why I wasn't the guy who sang it. I would explain about Identical Strangers and NewSong—I got blank stares. "So, you didn't sing it?"

At one station, they asked both of us about "Butterfly Kisses." Andy got up and left the interview. It got weird. There was too much to explain. News anchors didn't know what questions to ask me. "So. Let's see if I have this right: You're not Bob?"

I feel like I've been answering that question for twenty-five years.

---

* If Identical Strangers had ever done another record, I would have titled it *Big, Big, Day*.

The *Identical Strangers* record was really strong, in my opinion. Radio agreed. Audiences agreed. Yet, sales were low due to bonehead distribution: We were selling out in some markets where they couldn't get the record restocked. Meanwhile, Montana had plenty of copies gathering dust.

A combination of things got me to thinking. It was now 1996, and I was forty-one years old. Christian audiences are wonderful. They don't mind if you are aging. But touring is a young man's game. I knew enough about the music business to know that it would take two or three years to break in this new act. Did I really want to continue to do this? Yet again?

The success of "Butterfly Kisses" also seemed to dwarf *Identical Strangers*. (No offense intended to little people.) Lori and I prayed. Would my time be better spent at home writing songs? Damascus Road was crumbling. Buddy Killen's son-in-law, who was running the company, was now divorcing Buddy's daughter, who thought *she* was running the company. Buddy continued to sell what was left of his kingdom. Not a promising scenario!

I prayerfully concluded it was time to get out of the touring circus. What followed was classic. The "secular company" treated me honorably, and the Christian company put the screws to me. That's what you get for getting the name of your act from *Mad* magazine.

I asked Cal Turner to let me out of my deal. Done. Getting out of Damascus Road was a chore. It was further complicated by a fight between these two companies over

"A Father's Love." This was the song Bob and I penned to follow "Butterfly Kisses."

Buddy's son-in-law fought Cal IV for the song. I don't even remember what the outcome was. There was a lot going on that made me want to get out. I've never truly become a businessman, I guess. If you think "music business" is an oxymoron, try adding "Christian" to it! The rep for the Christian label showed no respect for my production abilities. I had become the golden goose songsmith that was leaving the flock.

I paid to get *out* of a record deal.

Looking back on my company days, I built major music catalogs at Maranatha, Lexicon, Word, PolyGram, Killen Music Group, and Cal IV (I've left out a few). These catalogs have been purchased (some multiple times) down through the years. Sony, Universal, and Warner Brothers gobbled them all up.

I don't know one single person with these companies who now owns my songs.

Songstory Writer Tip: Take a tip from Paul Overstreet, Bob Dylan, and others. Exploit your own songs. The old system was to get a big act to do your song. Those days are pretty much gone. If you write with a singer, release the song yourself with that singer. Got a band? Release the song yourself. Writers (like me) always whine about loss of ownership. Now they whine about the market being flooded.

Put your stuff out. There is a great market for those who are true amateurs. ("Amateur" means one who does it for love.) There's a niche for musicians who work the internet well. Learn from guys like Terry Taylor with D.A. or Scott Riggan. They get up every morning and market themselves.

Songstory XXII

Writing "Butterfly Kisses"

Try not to become a man of success.
Rather, become a man of value.
(Albert Einstein)

NOW I WANT to fly the Songstory time machine back to 1996. Pray for a good landing. We'll document the Thomas family story that has never been told. Until now. In contrast to the media hype, I submit that "Butterfly Kisses" would not have happened if Bob and I had not written "Surrender." That was the first Carlisle and Thomas song, and it still holds up. Between 1983 and 1993, we did life, family, and music together as partners. The post-ALLIES years (1993–1996) sent us off in different directions as we started to collaborate with outside writers.

Carlisle and Thomas were a strong team! Our very first country song "Why'd You Come in Here Lookin' Like That?" had been recorded by Dolly and gone straight to number one. Our compositions had been recorded by Hank Williams Jr., Ty England, Mel McDaniels, and others. We had a huge catalog of songs we had written and produced for Word Records with ALLIES. We built a country catalog with dozens of great songs that have (unfortunately) never been heard.

By 1996, the songwriting team became a non-exclusive deal. Bob had his solo contract with Diadem Records (later bought by Zomba). I had signed the aforementioned publishing deal with PolyGram music (later bought by Universal). Let's eavesdrop on what happened to bring about "Butterfly Kisses":

Bob came over to the studio in Franklin, Tennessee, from his house about a half mile away. He got out of his Jeep singing, "Big Rock Randy Mountain" (his descriptive song for our butter-yellow house that backed up to a forested hill).

Bob said, "I came over to warn you: Brookie has her license. She's driving now."

I laughed. "I'll stay off the roads, then. Crystal is going through that phase where she's not Daddy's little girl anymore. I'm gross now." We were both adjusting to the hard reality that our little girls were growing up. Bob nodded.

"I've got a song, man! The title is 'Butterfly Kisses'!" Bob unpacked his Gibson J45 that always smelled of Royal Copenhagen. He showed me a verse and chorus. It wasn't simple country music, nor was it pop. It wasn't unusual for Bob to have a great foundation. So much music was in place that the first thing to discuss was the story. (Story songs are harder to write than love songs, for sure.) It was about the love between a daddy and that daddy's girl. Bob was obviously thinking of his daughter Brooke, while I completely related the song to my oldest daughter, Crystal. (Randall and Sarah were still young enough to hug and hold.)

The second verse can make or break a song. It's the place where you need to approach the chorus from a new angle. With this in mind, I suggested, "In the second verse, how about she has her sixteenth-birthday party?" Bob was enthused. This made the repeating chorus into something new—calling for the pony and cake lyrics that are unique to the second chorus.

I tend to map things out to counter Bob's bursts of brilliance. It makes for a perfect songwriting storm. I suggested, "In the third verse, she gets married."

Bob recoiled, "Oh, no—I couldn't sing that! I'd wind up crying, man." Then he stopped. He got that "aha" look on his face; if it made Bob cry, maybe it would make *other* people cry! That is my memory of the first session. We put it on tape. Bob wrote "Butterfly Kisses" on a black cassette with a gold Sharpie. (I kept the tape.)

The next session was at Bob's house on Warrior Drive. Jacque called Lori. "You've got to hear this song that the guys are working on!" It was unusual that Jacque was so excited. I mean, we wrote songs all the time in those days. She had an objectivity that I didn't have.

There was another session in the studio at my house. The last snag was finishing up lines in the third verse. I think the last line written was "to perfume and makeup from ribbons and curls." We already had "trying her wings out in a great big world." It was like finishing the last part of a crossword puzzle. Done! Now, what did we have? Was this a Bob Carlisle song or a song to pitch in Nashville?

The answer came weeks later. Bob called. "Hi guy! I'm going to put 'Butterfly Kisses' on my record. Okay?" Well, of course it was okay. To be honest, I thought to myself, *Bob is with a small label. Maybe the best thing that can happen to that song is to have someone on a bigger label hear it.*

I was wrong about another artist being needed, because Bob treated the song with deep personal affection. He had the arrangement in his head. The key and tempo were set from the inception. Bob now became the producer. That was tricky. He needed to not over-produce it. To be a writer, arranger, background vocalist, lead vocalist, guitarist, programmer, and producer on the same song was asking too much—even if you are great at all those things.

Bob pulled it off.

A key part of the dynamic is that Bob and I were beginning to fear that our glory days were over. Bob had been cut from Sparrow Records to this smaller, unproven label. I was working on a lot of custom records. ("Custom" is a polite term for artists who sell their own records on a modest scale.) Our kids weren't starving. Yet. Our wives were probably wondering if we needed "straight" jobs. We were in our forties. Labels were signing embryos.

Diadem released "Butterfly Kisses" to the Christian market. It went up the charts to number two. There was a program director in Texas who refused to play the single unless someone wanted to buy him a new car. Argh.

The little label sent the song out to Adult Contemporary (secular) stations, and the reaction was astounding. Something really extraordinary was brewing. People flipped out! A couple of stations in Seattle and St. Louis claimed they "broke" "Butterfly Kisses," meaning they were the first to get the ball rockin'! The radio audience reacted big time. Fathers of little girls were sobbing. Mothers were asking where they could buy the song!

Meanwhile, Clive Calder at Jive Records was accidentally getting involved. He later relayed to me (in his lovely South African accent) that having acquired the Diadem label, he and his wife Patricia were having a last-minute listen to myriad CDs in his car.

They were arriving at a vacation spot, and they agreed that after "one more" song, they would stop listening and leave the music until they returned from their trip. She heard Bob sing a song ("On My Way to Paradise," by Carlisle and Thomas). That should have been the last song.

Amazingly, Patricia suggested, "Let's listen to just one more song."

Clive said, "All right. One more."

That "one more" song was "Butterfly Kisses." They let it play. Clive loved it. It touched him. He asked his wife, "What do you think?"

She didn't answer.

She was sobbing.

Clive said, "I immediately called my label execs and told them to put all our efforts behind this song. They didn't need much convincing; 'Butterfly Kisses' was burning things up on radio. I knew we had a major hit brewing! We wanted to be ready for the demand!"

A "Butterfly Kisses" frenzy began. The music industry never knows where lightning will strike next. What is wonderful about this song is that the demand came from LISTENERS! It was the people who made it explode: The dads and daughters of America decided that "Butterfly Kisses" would stay on top of the summer charts for *seven straight weeks!*

A Me-Too wave followed: The Raybon Brothers cut the song and threw it out to radio literally overnight! Jeff Carson put out his Curb Records CD with "Butterfly Kisses" as the title song. Even the legendary Sir Cliff Richard covered the song in Europe. "Besos de Mariposa" was the Spanish version in Latin countries. There were multiple competing parodies! There was even a detestable throbbing Euro dance version.

Country radio played three competing versions. This was like putting three jockeys on the same horse! Crazy. There are no benefits to having the same song rated at 11, 19, and 13. It's better to have one horse in the running. At least Bob's original version had the benefit of being viewed as the definitive one.

Bob was the writer, producer, and artist on what he called the *Shades of Grace* CD. This was quickly repackaged as *Butterfly Kisses.** It was really Bob's baby, so

---

* Word Records released a CD of ALLIES ballads with a large butterfly on the cover, titled *The Ballads of Bob Carlisle.* I was livid. Not only did they refuse years earlier to do an ALLIES Best Of, they also embarrassed themselves by obviously trying to cash in on the "Butterfly" buying spree, at the expense of their own artists' (ALLIES) integrity. Bad form!

when the record started heading for triple platinum status (three million units sold), there were three or four sources of income for him, which is the way it ought to be. I was a writer on four of the songs on the CD and on the single, so I was well rewarded with what songwriters call "mailbox money." PolyGram, as my publisher, took their half.

For every publishing (songwriters only) dollar, 50 cents went to PolyGram and 25 cents went to me. I had an advance debt of $80,000 or so. That got recouped first. Once it went in the black, the 25 percent started coming to Randy and Lori and the kids. (That's a sneaky way of saying we weren't wealthy, but we weren't poor, either...)

The song won three GMA Dove awards in Christian music. Three. It won the Nashville Area Award (Nammy) for Song of the Year 1998. There were ASCAP awards. The list goes on. It eclipsed all the other stuff we did. Bob's name will always be mentioned alongside the song.

My tombstone inscription may read, "Here Lies the Other Guy Who Wrote 'Butterfly Kisses.' " If "Butterfly Kisses" is what I'm remembered for when I'm dead ... I can live with that.

Songstory Writer Tip: Here's the tip you've all been waiting for. Every writer wants to know how his or her song can become a huge hit. The only people who claim to know are the ones trying to sell you something.

There is no easy answer. It happens in different ways for different people.

Let's look at what usually happens before a hit song:

A writer composes a bunch of lame songs. Then the writer determines to get better. The writer learns to co-write. The writer learns to re-write. The writer becomes proficient on an instrument. The writer moves to Nashville, L.A., or New York.

The writer works with established writers. The writer works with established artists. The writer generates cuts as an artist. The writer produces and/or engineers recordings. The writer composes both on demand *and* by design. The writer eventually develops a catalog of published songs.

The writer sees his or her songs performed live on television. The writer hears his or her compositions while in a restaurant in Fort Myers called Mission BBQ. The writer is credited on songs with co-writers who the writer has never met. Parodies are made of the writer's best songs. The writer receives royalties for songs the writer *doesn't even remember.*

Somewhere along the way, a song hits. Then possibly another. This is how it works. *Songwriters work.*

Posers skip these steps.

Have you done all these things? Really? If so, I'd like to meet you. We should lunch.

Songstory XXIII

Did You Help Me Write This Song?

Those in power write the history,
while those who suffer write the songs.
(Frank Harte)

A good story trumps the truth.
(Songstory)

MASTERING IS THAT final process where a mumbling mad-scientist engineer who has never heard your project puts the final sheen on the product. Bob called. "We're mastering at Georgetown. Come on out, man!" (Georgetown owner/engineer Denny Purcell was a lovable genius. RIP.)

"Sure, bud! I'll be there with bells on." I showed up without bells, because I couldn't find any that matched my T-shirt.

It was fantastic hearing "Butterfly Kisses" with the final touches, ready for release. While we listened, Bob said, "Hey, man, help me out—did you help me write this song?"

I'm not sure if I veiled my shock. This didn't sound like Bob. I stiffened. "Yes. You don't remember?"

The song continued to play. Bob apologized. I probed to find out where this unprecedented question came from. I said, "I know you've worked hard on this song. Did you not want to split this 50/50?"

Bob waved it off. "Oh, no—50/50 like always."

There was nothing in my memory banks to compare this to. I recounted the conversation to Lori at home. She said, "*WHAT*? He doesn't remember all those times you guys worked on it?" I had to shrug it off.

It was harder to shrug off the next episode. When "Butterfly Kisses" started to hit, Bob and I were nominated for a Gospel Music Association (GMA) Dove award. Lori and I received our invitation in the mail. I think it was $150 a seat; it would cost $300 for Lori and me to attend the awards. It felt extravagant spending that much renting two seat cushions. We had three kids to feed. "Let's not," I said. How was I to know what was going to happen?

Lori and I were invited by worship leaders Wayne and Rachel Tate* to come over and watch the Dove Awards on their big screen. Lori and I didn't have cable, so it was a nice gesture on their part. A group of church friends gathered with us. It was fun thinking that the show we were watching was happening a few miles up the road. We also knew most of the Christian music artists and executives who looked so uncomfortable in their gowns and tuxes.

---

* Wayne Tate was nearly crushed to death between two automobiles when this book was being written. Wayne miraculously survived. DUDE! We are praying that you heal up well, buddy.

The Song of the Year was saved until later in the broadcast. "The winner this year is ... BUTTERFLY KISSES!" Our little group started jumping up and down. The ladies were screaming. Our song played. Bob came up. He thanked Ray Ware and his label. They did the walk-off. The screen went to a commercial. That living room in Franklin went silent. Everyone looked at Lori and me. They were horrified. No one knew what to say. Wayne broke the silence with one syllable. He looked at me with hurt in his eyes and exclaimed, "DUDE!"

Frantic phone calls started coming to the Tate house from friends on the floor at the Dove Awards. "Where are you guys? You've got to get down here!" Lori and I drove up to the show, and we were let in by special dispensation. I was told to follow Bob around while the media interviewed him and to take photos. This was in order to be the "me-too" songwriter for "Butterfly Kisses." I was the silent guy like Penn and Teller. A gaggle of media who knew Bob as the man of the moment were firing questions. Bob introduced me. That ended the interview. Awkward. And the weird was about to get weirder.

The Thomases and Carlisles had been best buddies. The four of us against the music business. Now, the Carlisle house became Butterfly Kisses Central. Plus, Bob and Jacque had begun a major home renovation. Banging and clanging. George King and Ray Ware used the dining room as a War Room. Media strategies. Book deals. Tour offers. The ranch house became a madhouse.

Bob Carlisle became *the* in-demand public figure overnight. The song was a sensation. Everyone was Bob's new best friend. Except his old best friend.

There were no calls coming to the Thomas house. Why? The rumor around Nashville was that the lucky "co-writer" had written only one line of the song.

One.

Line.

I tracked down the rumor. It came from the War Room. I mistakenly thought that such a major hit song meant good news for everybody. The "One Line" story caused Nashville insiders to view me as an enviable guy who got rich for doing nothing. People outside the loop tended to see an unknown co-writer as braggart at best and liar at worst. Friends were asking me if I felt angry. My answer was "No, I would describe the feeling as *empty*."

Buddy Killen empathized with my experience. The wise mogul in the ivory tower had seen it all. He said, "Sometimes life hands you a hollow victory that reminds you that God and family are more important than your career." Buddy nailed it. "A hollow victory." The hollowed-out feeling would hang over me for years.

Gordon Kennedy understood. He had a credit issue on the huge hit "Change the World." Three guys wrote it. But years had passed. Gordon's two friends were set to share the songwriter income when it hit. Gordon was left out. He had to raise a little ruckus. Afterwards, all three were correctly listed. These things happen. But that don't make it right.

Things got even wilder at the Carlisle house. Bob and family appeared on the *Oprah Winfrey Show.* Oprah held up the CD and simply said, "Buy this." Tens of thousands of viewers obeyed.

After some of these appearances, Bob would return home and apologize to me for not mentioning his old partner. The canard developed that Bob Carlisle had written the song one night for his daughter Brooke. Bob was quoted as saying, "The song poured out of me, almost in its entirety one night."

I get it. A good story trumps the truth. The media embraces the fairy tale. A doting father wrote this song for his little girl. A tearful nation said, "Aw..." That goes well with the song. It probably even helped sell it. There was some truth there—Bob certainly was always devoted to little Brookie.

The story from *my* family's point of view was that a seasoned songwriter team had been blessed by God. Hoping to write "someone's favorite song," they carefully crafted "Butterfly Kisses" in multiple sessions. (Boring!) Randy was thinking of his two beautiful daughters, Crystal and Sarah. (Confusing!) The problems with my family's story were that it was mundane and we didn't have the megaphone.

You gotta make hay while the iron is hot. Major book deals for Bob were cemented quickly. So quickly that stories of daddy and daughters were compiled. Absent was the Randy and Crystal story.

A Father's Love book came later. It included Ray and his son. George King and his son. Conspicuous by its absence was a Randy and Randall story. It was surreal for my kids. We tried to keep the books away and turn the radio off. Lori's anger turned to a deep sadness.

The fairy tale "Butterfly Kisses" narrative was no friend to me. On a cloudy winter afternoon, I was walking on Main Street in Franklin. Two kids from Franklin Classical School recognized me. We were standing in front of the historic Franklin Theatre.

"Mister Thomas, we heard that you helped write that song 'Butterfly Kisses.' Is that true?"

I was precise in my response. "Yes, I co-wrote the song with my friend Bob Carlisle. We worked on it at our house."

They lit up. "You mean, that house where Crystal, Randall, and Sarah live?"

"Yes." Their eyes rounded out like marbles.

The mom walked up to join us asking, "What are ya'll talking about?"

Her children said, "Mister Thomas here was telling us he helped write 'Butterfly Kisses'—in Sarah's house!"

Her brow furrowed. "No, he didn't. Bob Carlisle wrote that song!" She gathered up her kids like a hen with her chicks and walked them away from me across Main Street. She shot a stern look over her shoulder that said, *"You ought to be ashamed of yourself."*

Similar conversations took place in California and Florida. When someone introduces me as a co-writer on "Butterfly Kisses," I brace for impact. The response is usually, "Really? Wait. I thought Bob Carlisle wrote that song." That's the routine.

(I'm typing this in the summer of 2021. A lady approached me last night. "So, you are Bob?"

I answered, "No, I'm Randy."

"Oh. Someone told me you wrote 'Butterfly Kisses.'")

The most unfortunate fallout has been with my daughters. Crystal had to explain to her friends about all of the above. She didn't get to be the Butterfly Girl. (Which she actually is, to me.) Crystal was sometimes teased with that term.

People automatically assume my daughters had "Butterfly Kisses" in their weddings. *Au contraire!* (That's French for, "You know what happens when we assume.") When Crystal married her husband Brandon, she made it clear that "Butterfly Kisses" would *not* in any way be included in her wedding.

My youngest daughter Sarah married Jeff Harvey. They surprised me with their choice for the father/daughter dance at her wedding: She chose "I Wish I Could" by Colin Raye. (Apologies to the Peabo Bryson version.) I was so happy to dance with Sarah to her song.

"Butterfly Kisses" was *not* a happy experience for my family.

It was happy for millions of other families, though. There was a moment here in Naples, Florida, when I was singing "Butterfly Kisses" for a father of the bride dance. The father and I locked eyeballs for a brief moment. It was pretty great. Moments like these are what the song is all about.

I hope my family's disconnect doesn't diminish anyone's enjoyment of "Butterfly Kisses" as a song. It is heartfelt. Bob really feels it. It's all the business stuff that gets weird. Why? Because we're all sinners. I probably should have had a blowout confrontation with Bob. My wife says I never stick up for myself. I kept my mouth shut.

I said to Lori, "I'm going to write a book someday."

Bob overheard. He yelled out, "Oh, *now* I'm in trouble!"

So I've let twenty-some years go by. There's a truckload of hindsight now. Who wants to read about a songwriter complaining about not getting credit? You want some cheese to go with that whine? Don Henley would sneer, "Get over it!" It's not like I need to join a Grumpy Grammy Winner support group.

In order to help process the joy and sadness that "Butterfly Kisses" brought, I think of it like there are three Bobs. Bob One was the youthful, dynamic sweetheart who sang his guts out. My songwriting partner. He always said, "I'll always be grateful for ALLIES yanking me out of Club World." Bob Three is a sweet guy who lives with his beloved Jacque in Orange County, California. He is Frampa to the grandkids. He says, "It was nice being rich. I wish I'd taken more pictures!"

In between was Bob Two: the face of "Butterfly Kisses" videos. He was the millionaire who lived the country club life in Las Vegas. Bob Two struggled against becoming a One Hit Wonder. There were very dark years that followed the Butterfly limelight. Bob Two had watched millions of dollars sprout wings and fly away. This is the Bob who said to me, "I've been to the mountaintop. There's nothing up there but sniper fire."

There's a soft spot in my head for all three Bobs. One of my favorite early memories is of Bob being a Denny's customer. There was a waitress working the counter that morning. She was obviously big pregnant. She walked as if her feet hurt. The way she supported herself while pouring coffee indicated some back pain. The long-haired Bob put on his hat and left quietly. On the counter, the check and payment were tucked under the plate. There was something else there, too. Call it a tip.

It was a hundred-dollar bill.

Songstory Writer Tip: If you are a singer who writes, you have an advantage. Singers like to avoid consonants. Words like "watchstrap" don't sing well. I heard Petra onstage singing a song titled "Occupy." It was jarring to my ear. They even pause after the "Oc" (oc-cupy). I pictured a giant octopus. (Love Petra. Hate the song.) Perhaps it's an '80s thing.

Vowels are our friends. I've gravitated to titles like "Valerie" or "You Led Me to Believe." Bryan Duncan is still singing that last one and trying to explain why I wrote it! I've never written a song with Englebert Humperdinck's name in it. Gretchen is a very un-singable name, unless you are Donald Fagan trying to make people like me laugh.

If you sing well, make your inner rock star happy. Write stuff that soars easily. If you are a writer who admits you can't sing, get a singer's input. If some of your lyrics trip up a singer on a demo, it's going to keep your song from being sung by a pro (like Englebert Humperdinck).

Songstory XXIV

The Goodbye Look
(Won't You Pour Me a Cuban Breeze, Gretchen?*)

*Stab the body and it heals, but injure the heart,
and the wound lasts a lifetime.*
(Mineko Iwasaki)

Butterfly Haze

EACH DAY AFTER "Butterfly Kisses" was better than
the next. (You may want to read that sentence again.)
Writing with Bob was no longer a collaboration of equals.
He was the Butterfly Boy, and I wasn't. Songs had to be
Bob's idea. Had to fit the celebrity criteria. My ideas were
shot down. With maximum interference and minimum
fun, we managed to write "A Father's Love."

We wrote a few other things. But the fun ended soon
after the big hit. We had grown up writing for the joy of
it. Now the Grammy taunted the new songs. "You think
you can beat me? Not likely." It was a three-way write:
Bob, me, and the song we had to outdo. I put up with it
out of love for Bob. The angelic muse had had enough,

---

* From Donald Fagan's "The Goodbye Look."

211

though. She refused to be in the same room with us and That Song.

We soldiered on, in a Butterfly Haze.

That winter, "A Father's Love" was included in the movie *Jack Frost* starring Michael Keaton and Kelly Preston. There was a screening with most of the Christian music crowd in attendance. The Jars of Clay guys sat nearby (they had a song in the movie as well). The hero of the film is a starving musician. Kelly Preston played the wife. She has a line that hit home with this Nashville audience: "I don't have any money. My husband is a musician!"

"A Father's Love" was placed after most of the end credits rolled. You know, when theaters are empty. Bob said, "I imagined the guy sweeping up popcorn going, 'Hm. Nice song'…"

I have uncomfortable memories of subsequent co-writes on the *Stories from the Heart* record. Reba McEntire's Starstruck studio was at Bob's command. There was access to a roof on Starstruck. That's when we really left our mark on Nashville: Bob brought his spud chucker, and we shot potatoes at all the surrounding buildings. Sorry, Reba. (RCA studio B, you should check your roof.)

In a side studio, a programmer was feverishly putting a track together. A main studio was humming with musicians to add the human elements. Bob escorted me down the hall and warned me, "This is important, man. This isn't one of your little Identical Strangers records." That stung.

It was a three-ring circus. Everything was high dollar and high pressure. Bob closed me in a room, saying, "The sooner you get me lyrics, the sooner I can go sing it."

I used a pencil. I figured there wasn't time to let the ink dry. I was promoted back to co-writer. To save time. This was the closest I came to walking out on Bob. I stuck it out. I'd sold circus tickets before.

"Butterfly Kisses" Killed the Songwriting Team That Created It

My poor wife, Lori. She had to console me after days of being a subordinate copy boy. She nursed me through the times in Bob's career when I traveled as substitute for Bob's sound man. I would set up a stage and monitors for Bob hours before a gig. Bob would come in to sing and then head back to a hotel. I would go to a Denny's with a church staff member and a lighting guy. I was Bob's crew. Often, none of the promoters knew I was an ALLIES alumnus or even a musician. But being humbled is a good thing.

Instead of opening up, our little circus got smaller. There were fewer writing sessions. Our tax accountant advised me to stop working. My extra income from producing records and running Radio Ranch studio was all going to the IRS.

Bob's circus got bigger. He and George King started Butterfly Music Group. I'm sure Bob could write a bitter book about BMG. They built a business complex and began acquiring music catalogs. The whole thing went horribly wrong and hemorrhaged money. Lawsuits came along years later.

In recent years, I asked Bob, "Do you ever look back and wonder where all the money went?"

He answered tersely, "I know where every single penny went."

I think that writing with Bob became an exercise in futility. Treating a co-writer as an assistant doesn't work. In the interest of friendship, I needed to stay away from the Butterfly Circus. It was time to face the unvarnished truth: "Butterfly Kisses" killed the songwriting team that created it.

Carlisle and Thomasongs was over.

Bob and Jacque moved to Vegas. File that under "I Didn't See That Coming." Bob said if anyone needed to get in touch, he could mail a letter addressed:

Bob.

Vegas.

The heavily modified Carlisle house went up for sale. Along with it went the memory of two families joined by a band called ALLIES and the room where "Butterfly Kisses" was forged.

Our church friend, Janine Farro, had a family with five kids. They needed a big house. Lori put the Farros in touch with the Carlisles. The Farros wished they could afford the large ranch house with all the modern ameni-ties. Bob got on the phone with Wayne Farro. The baby was playing on Wayne's lap. The prospect of buying the Carlisle house looked hopeless. There was a six-figure difference between the fair market value of the Warrior Drive property and what the family could afford.

Bob said, "What's your baby's name?"

Wayne answered, "Isabel."

Bob heard the baby cooing. He was touched. He said, "You can have the house."

The Warrior Drive house became a second home again for my kids. In that same room where "Butterfly Kisses" was written, two of the young Farro boys learned how to play guitar and drums. Their names are Josh and Zac Farro. My son Randall was singing some amazing vocals with them.

Josh borrowed an ESP Les Paul–shaped guitar of mine. I guess some guitars are like royalty. Meant to live a life of glory. That ESP was an infantry pawn. It got beaten and scarred. It came back like a wounded vet. I said, "What happened? You've changed, man. I don't even know you anymore." That ESP had PTSD. Sad. I had to burn it to put it out of my misery.

The Farros started a band called Paramore. The teenagers certainly developed skills. Twenty years later, I read about their infighting after huge successes. Sound familiar? We're all a mess, aren't we? I wonder who is using that music room today on Warrior Drive. Do they know the Butterfly/Paramore history in that house?

I can see now that God was using the whole "Butterfly Kisses" hollowness to teach me a lot of things. Who do you turn to for answers? Psalm 34:15 says, "The eyes of the LORD are on the righteous, and his ears are attentive to their cry." (Christ is my righteousness.)

The songwriting profession began to take on a different appearance. It looked like a part of my past, along with my songwriting partnership. God was stirring something up. I had seen it before, when we left California. There was a day when California gave me the Goodbye Look. Charming Franklin (where we raised our kids!) would one day become a part of our past. Now Nashville was giving us the Goodbye Look.

Many years after the crazy Oprah days, Bob and I talked on the phone. He apologized for not mentioning his co-writer when the Butterfly searchlight lit him up. Something happened in my inmost being. I heard Bob's heart and felt the godly sorrow that he expressed and applied it to the entire "Butterfly Kisses" partner-becomes-copy-boy misadventure. Our Carlisle and Thomas account was squared up right then and there. Jesus said, "If you forgive others their trespasses, your heavenly Father will also forgive you" (Matthew 6:14).

Selah.

There's forgiveness that comes with forgiveness. Bob sang a song about it. I Googled it and found it on cancioneros.com. "Forgiveness" was written by Rick Crawford and me. Are you ready for this? They have the lyrics that I wrote with Rick. They are credited to Rick Crawford and John Feldman! You gotta laugh.

I'll close this chapter with some fool's wisdom: You'll find that the older you get, the more birthdays I've had. The older I get, the more Ricky Gervais looks like Bob Carlisle. The older Bob gets, the more I look like Liam

Neesom. From the back. Have you ever seen the four of us in the same room? Hm. Makes you wonder…

Songstory Writer Tip: When writing with a collaborator, check your ego at the door. You need to be able to throw out ideas without fear of getting shot down. The process often works with a writer coming up with an idea that may be half-baked. The co-writer responds with something else, and that Third Thing emerges. If songwriters trust each other completely, this leads to great stuff. There's an old miner's saying in Nashville, "You've got to move a lot of dirt to get to the gold."

Always treat your co-writer as an equal. "Freely you have received; freely give." One day you're being mentored. Another day you become the mentor. Great songs are written while the writers value one another. When ego takes over, inspiration takes a hike.

I wish somebody had told me that.

Songstory XXV

Getting the Band
Back Together

The class reunion has been postponed another year.
Everyone is trying to lose another ten pounds.
(Greeting card)

Legacy artists. It's a polite way of saying "old."
Songstory

THERE'S SOMETHING IN human nature that demands reunions. I attended my ten-year high school bash. Quarterback of the football team? Bald, unemployed. Head cheerleader? Overweight, selling insurance. Student body president? Unsuccessful gay script writer in North Hollywood. Band drum major (me)? Traveling Jesus Freak. That was the last class reunion for me. But many band reunions were in my future.

The year 2001 was a banner year. Sweet Comfort Band was invited by Street Level Artists to do summer dates with a "Legends of CCM" package. Legends? Hardly. There was another name they called us: Legacy artists. It's a polite way of saying "old." The other "legacy" bands were the 77s and Daniel Amos. The venues were all major Christian festivals. With computer technology, I was able to communicate with the old band mates via email. SCB rehearsals were held in Riverside.

Bryan had continued his solo career in the ensuing decades since Sweet C. But now, the only way he could get on these big festivals was to succumb to returning to SCB as a legacy (oldies) act. Secular music respects its elders. The Christian music industry expects to get its wisdom from the young.

Rick had spent decades building a construction business, but bashing on a drum set is kind of a young man's game. And if Rick was pushing fifty, Bryan was dragging it! (*My apologies to Mr. Five-Foot-Four and Three-Quarters. I'm always kidding him. Back in the day, he would ask me for money, and I would chide him, "What's the matter? You a little SHORT?"*)

Kevin had to dust off his bass. You don't think about warming up or staying in shape when you're young. The Rocky Balboa "Gonna Fly Now" theme was playing (but only in our heads). I was traveling with guitars supplied by ESP that had no connection to the Sweet C. days. I had a soul patch growing below my lip that said, "I may be old, but at least I'm not relevant!"

The songs were very nostalgic for all of us. And muscle memory really is a thing. I don't think any of us needed to do the concerts for money. Maybe we did it to see if we could still do it! Bryan, the backslidden piano player, had to actually play again. Yeah, I think he was surprised. He would watch his hands working, like, "Hey, I used to be pretty good!"

Festival dates are big affairs. Hard to get in and hard to get out. The band did its thing very well. But it was just part of a touring package, which means there wasn't enough demand for any of the three bands to actually stand alone.

I had seen package tours with Foreigner, Peter Frampton, and REO Speedwagon. So, I guess there's no shame in needing three old acts to get us on big stages. It enabled us to meet fans. And Sweet Comfort Band fans are the best. I mean it. Some drove from surrounding states just to see us. Those are the people I was so honored to meet. The kind of people who will read Songstory!

There were no plane crashes or major mishaps on our reunion tour. There is one story worth telling: Randy Stonehill joined us for some of the appearances. We were playing Cornerstone Festival outside of Chicago (the home of Rez Band). During Stonehill's set, he called up Larry Norman. These were two of the original Jesus Music icons. There had been good beginnings and bad blood between Stonehill and Norman, so everyone knew this was a moment in Christian Rock History. We watched from backstage and cried. You can't outrun God's grace.

Pastor Vincent's Aging Farts Club Band

John and Cherie Roberts are buddies who go back to the Sunrise days. In 2000, Cherie and I talked on the phone and caught up on about twenty years of adventures. Cherie said, "This was so fun! We should have a reunion!"

I said, "Let's pray about it."

Cherie asked, "On the phone?"

I smiled. "Why not?"

And that began a Koinonia reunion. Not because I prayed with Cherie, but because (as my wife says) *women make things happen!*

Our buddy Rick Schneblin began an email/phone campaign. I recorded a spoof song using the Sgt. Pepper's theme. I redid the song as "Pastor Vincent's Aging Farts Club Band." I also did a "Come Together" remake as a call to join the reunion and do a lyrical "roast" of the band Sonrise. Schneblin turned it into a great video.

Jaymes Felix put together equipment. We gathered at the original San Bernardino Community Church. It hadn't changed much. (The '70s yellow and orange colors had been toned down a bit.) The people running the church had never heard of any of us!

Aging Jesus Freaks made a pilgrimage from around California, Tennessee, Ohio, Oregon, and as far away as Holland. We had Mike Hodge, Jaymes, Matt Chapman, Sam Scott, Vince Neypes, John Roberts, Randy Lee, and others. We sang old Psalm 150 songs and Andraé songs and whatever we could think of. We "testified" like in the old days—but now people had decades of wisdom and news to impart.

It was one of the greatest home-grown events of my life. There was so much hugging and crying going on. It was a delight to see all the old crowd and to sing and pray and laugh together again.

Forget high school reunions. Go do a reunion with your old youth group!

Sonrise at Radio Ranch

The Sonrise dinosaurs converged on Radio Ranch (Big Rock Randy Mountain) in the winter of 2004. Michael Hodge, Steve Latanation, Matt Chapman, and I were all in the Nashville area. Sam drove down from Ohio and John Roberts came from California. I set us up to record. As we picked up our instruments, we discovered we had been separated for so long that we didn't remember any of our old songs. None.

We blew through Neil Young, Cream, and Beatles-era songs. The band sounded better as old guys than we did when we were young. It sounded better than the original band because Steve had become a great singer!

The band took a photo under the Sonrise macramé rug that had adorned our commune back in 1974. I love them boys.

Bruce's Birthday Bash (I Got Nuthin' Tour '05)

In November of 2005, we got most of the original ALLIES lineup back together. Our buddy Gregg Hodge asked us to surprise his brother Bruce for a "birthday bash." Big, big, day. We had Jimmy Erickson, Sam, Matt, and me (Bob had to bow out). Joining on lead vocals was a young Florida pastor, Charles Thomas. It had been a dozen years since I had played ALLIES songs. Plus, I must have written too many songs in the meantime.

Someone thought it was a good idea to play only songs from the first record. They neglected to tell me. Hoping it would help, I pulled out the old Valley Arts guitar that I used on the old records. Unfortunately, I was totally stumped at the rehearsal. There was a point when everyone stopped and looked at me, wondering why I wasn't soloing and holding up my end. I came up with the reunion catch-phrase when I threw up my hands and admitted, "I got nuthin'!"

We played unannounced at the Franklin Mercantile. It was a complete surprise to birthday boy Bruce. The customers who were there had no idea what was going on. Dino Elefante stopped by. I'll bet there are hundreds of old ALLIES fans who would've loved to hear that reunion. I think we were pretty good. Chuck's vocals were very impressive. Very few singers can successfully tread where Bob Carlisle has trod.

Sweet Comfort Band reunited again in 2015 for some great nights at The Upper Room in Mission Viejo, California. Bob even sang backing vocals on one occasion. I remember Bryan saying, "I've been kicked out of a lot of churches, but I've never been kicked out of Jesus."

I wonder if that's not entirely accurate. I bet some churches have asked him politely to leave.

Songstory Writer Tip: Remember your basic training.

Look up the song "Hey, Joe" by Hendrix. The chords are C, G, D, A, E.

These five chord shapes can be used all over the neck. You intermediate players probably already bar the E and A shape (the A shape on the fifth fret becomes D). Learn to bar your C shape (this is advanced stuff) and your D shape to open up loads of new possibilities. I think the G shape is trickier. I use that in partial form—don't try to bar it. You'll get cramps.

When you master this stuff, you can play a given chord at any location in the neck. A master guitarist uses his ABCs every day.

Keyboardists—play a C triad, CEG (low to high). Boring. Now GCE. Stronger. EGC. Nice with the root on top. Now play B-flat over C; C over E; A-flat over C. Notice the "leading tone" to these. These are chords that want to go somewhere. Play F over C; D over C. These have tension. They want to resolve. Play G over C. Pleasant, but vacant. Just messing with triads can teach you about how chords can convey emotions. These can be incredible tools when writing music. Play GDF (low to high). Now resolve it to GCE. Tension/resolution—that's the intro to "Butterfly Kisses."

Songstory XXVI

The Conversion Inside
the Conversion

*Just one sentence from you would have been a great gift,
but you have given me a waterfall of truth in
the pages of sacred Scripture.*
(*From a prayer in* Killing Calvinism *by Greg Dutcher*)

The Life-Giving Words of Dead Men

THE TWILIGHT YEARS of the twenty-first century brought a rebirth to the old Jesus Freak. My faith had become a ragged quilt of Jesus Movement ideals with Baptist, Assembly of God, Foursquare, and recent Presbyterian patches. It had been a comfortable blanket of inter-denominational non-denominationalism. It wasn't comfortable anymore. There were too many conflicting ideas in my head. (God smiled.)

I think I tried to be open to anything. For a moment, I tried to be an atheist. (God laughed.) I read some "spiritual" books. Perhaps Kahlil Gibran influences would help me be individualistic, so as not to be labeled along with televangelists? (God drummed His fingers.) All right, then. Let's learn some history and put the ancient texts of the Bible in context. (God rubbed His palms together.)

The headmaster of Franklin Classical School was Dr. George Grant. We had dozens of his humanities lectures on cassettes. These helped with much of my missing education. I dipped into the well of the Church fathers. Clement, Ignatius, and Polycarp wrote in a similar style to the New Testament. Patrick of Ireland (ironically a Brit!) surprised me with his mysticism. He would have made a good Pentecostal (unlike me).

Augustine of Hippo thought big thoughts. During the fall of the Roman Empire, he had written *The City of God* as an explanation of the permanence of the Church against the ebbs and tides of the cyclical City of Man. Wycliff, Hus, and others sowed seeds of change. A rotund German monk named Luther was used as a tipping point in church history. Martin would have changed the song "Shout to the Lord" into "Fart at the Devil."

The French lawyer Calvin organized much of the resulting Christian thought. He didn't have a good publicist. Calvin's history has been written by his enemies. There were Knox, Cranmer, Edwards, and so many others through whom God's work continued. For years I read only the life-giving words of dead men.

All of these influences threw new light on how the Scriptures have shaped my thinking. I began to *think*. It hurt only at first. God enabled me to read the Bible in a new way. I wanted to read the Bible to help me understand the commentaries. The commentary of a great cloud of witnesses was actually a great help.

I reread God's Word as if for the first time. It was unchanged, while I was not. The black and white turned to Technicolor again. The Fall of mankind jumped out from nearly every printed page. The sovereignty of God hovered over the work. The Spirit of God breathed life into every line. The Father of lights showed in the narrative. And Christ became truly God and truly man.

The conversion inside my conversion was unexpected. What was happening to me? I expected my new approach to faith to be totally unique. I was wrong. Checking in with Scotty Smith and Mike Smith at Christ Community Church in Franklin, the response was, "Yes, we've been teaching these things all along." Really? Why couldn't I hear it before? The scales fell. I had been deaf, and now I could see!

It was during this time that Lori and I sang and played in the worship band at Christ Community Church. Worship leader David Hampton had the finest Nashville musicians and singers at his disposal. He also had me. I say that because it was a challenge to keep up with that level of excellence. I had spent my life making up my own parts. It's another discipline to read a chart and serve someone else's arrangement. Guitarist Rex Paul Schnelle helped me navigate the notation.

On an Easter Sunday, David had a fantastic program put together. A powerful spring storm blew through Franklin that morning and cut the power to the city. Industrious ladies ran off to find candles. The other guitarist handed me an acoustic instrument. There were no screens, no lights, no P.A. Only two guitars. I don't remember what we sang, but I do remember what Pastor Scotty Smith said after Easter services were over.

Scotty (who had a habit of making up words) bounded onto the platform and exclaimed, "That was wonderful! Let's do this again next year! We'll do the whole service PIGGLIAGATTO!"

The Jesus Freak Had Been Reformed

Lori and I attended George Grant's class on Sunday morning. Amy Grant and Vince Gill came to class. Everyone thankfully treated Amy and Vince as if they were not famous. Hey, there were lots of famous musicians in that class. I wondered if Vince had ever been exposed to George's enthusiastic reformed teaching. Wouldn't you know it? Vince and Amy showed up for the class on Election. This is a tough theological nut to crack, but Dr. Grant did not hold back the full force of the scriptural truth.

I don't know what Vince had been exposed to before this. Amy had been to CCC for years. Did they get their minds blown? I know I did, but I was well braced for it. Lori whispered to me, "I wonder if we'll see Amy and Vince in the class next week?"

We never saw them again. To be fair, they might have left on tour. Or perhaps they elected* not to return?

You could shake a stick at all the books that Dr. George Grant has written, but your hand would get tired. George was a challenging mentor to me. And Nate Larkin was a buddy. Nate is a recovering preacher's kid who became

---

* Pastor Byron West contributed this witticism.

a pastor. He formed a ministry known as The Samson Society. Pirate monks (see Nate's book, *Samson and the Pirate Monks*) were often seen gathering at McCreary's on Main and wandering the streets of Franklin. I witnessed countless other men getting their hearts refreshed.

The Jesus Freak had been reformed. It's like being born again *again*. How can I express this new outpouring of grace? I began to write worship songs. Again. I was asking God, "How can I serve the church?" Which begs the question, "Well, who am I?" If you boil it down—I'm a Christian/musician. What can a Christian musician do? Answer: Be a worship leader!

I spoke with David Hampton about the possibility of serving as a worship leader. He must have been connected. (Or as George Patton would say, "He stands in good with the Lord.") From that one conversation, a number of pastors called me from around the country. We were flown to different states to interview with churches.

What if we could find something in our own back yard? There were some exciting conversations with George Grant about a church plant. Those plans were postponed. (It later became Parish Presbyterian in Franklin.) There was a pastor named George "Bing" Davis who had just returned from Naples, Florida (where millionaires are middle class). Christ Community and Bing were talking about planting a church in Spring Hill. Spring Hill? That was practically our back yard!

A new chapter was about to begin. (Double entendre intended.)

Songstory Writer Tip: Play your great song for a person who doesn't like you. If everyone likes you, try to find a good critic. Good critics are hard to find, but their feedback is like gold. Anytime a good critic says, "I don't like that first part," then throw out the first part. Anytime a good critic says, "I only like this one line, here," keep that one line.

Very few of you will take this advice. And do you know why? Because you have no objectivity about your song. You want to keep your song the way you like it. You would rather the whole world change its taste to match yours. It ain't gonna happen. A good critic represents something your song desperately needs: An audience.

Songstory XXVII

Grace Fellowship and the Dead Cat

Everyone said they were crazy.
Brenda, you know you're much too lazy,
and Eddie could never afford to live that kind of life.
Ah, but there we were wavin' Brenda and Eddie goodbye.
(Billy Joel)

If you close the door on God, the Holy Spirit
comes innuendo.
(Songstory)

Boom Town

BROTHER, SPRING HILL was a-boomin' in the early 2000s. There was some booming in Spring Hill during the Civil War. Essentially, the Rebel Army was spoiling for a fight. They found the dang Yankees in Spring Hill one afternoon. It was purt-near sundown, so they fired off some cannons and yelled disparaging remarks about Yankee mamas to warn those Johnnies they'd get whooped good come morning.

Both armies settled in to sleep, knowing they would have a battle at first light. That's how you're supposed to do it. But the Union Army tiptoed away in their jammies as the Billy Rebs slept. Those Rebs were mad as hornets the next morning. Nothing angers Confederates more than yellow blue-bellies.

The Union fellas tucked their tails and slithered up to Franklin. The Rebels had to catch up the next day, which meant the Battle of Franklin started behind schedule. The Yankees repeated the whole middle-of-the night tip-toe escape scenario. That led to the battle of Nashville, which pretty much decimated the Confederate Army of Tennessee.

The Tennessee town maps are still based around nineteenth-century wagon trails and country roads. But in the twentieth century, some of the locals started picking banjos and yodeling with a nasal twang. Things got a whole lot better, for a while. Then them dang Yankees started invading Nashville. Again.

I Might Have Been Knighted

In 2002, our Christ Community buddies gave us a "called-into-ministry" ceremony. Dr. Grant even brought out a Scottish sword and touched me on the head and shoulders during a very rich Presbyterian commissioning prayer. I might actually have been knighted. I'm not sure.

On the way from historic Franklin to Spring Hill, you pass though Thompson Station. In those days, you might miss it. We would find our way around based on where things used to be. (You remember where Johnson's still blew up? Well, that's where you turn.) There were the refurbished remains of a train station that housed the

Thompson Station Grill. This was the birthplace of Grace Fellowship.

Lori and I began leading worship for forty people at the station. It was casual. Mike Sligar was a record company marketing guy who helped us quite a bit. We started with a staff of two: Pastor Bing Davis and me.

We quickly grew and moved to Heritage Middle School. Every Sunday was a full setup and teardown—church in a trailer. I was elected by our congregation to be an elder. They figured I had some sense. Well, I'm only 'bout half stupid, so they were 'bout half right.

Being an elder and "elding" is a big deal, since it is a biblical office. It is said that when James Garfield became president, he left his position as an elder in the church saying, "I resign the highest office in the land to become president of the United States." My kind of guy.

For four years, I served as worship leader and ruling elder. As worship leader, I learned to choose the songs and plan the worship well, so that I could ignore the complaints. As a pastor once told me, "A preacher can give a great sermon or a terrible sermon, and very few churchgoers will notice the difference. But everyone will have an opinion about the music!" I did some touring with SheDaisy and Paul Brandt in those days. Brian Fullen was the drummer in both cases. They were smaller jaunts, so Brian could keep up with studio dates, and I could work for the church.

The Taste of Betrayal

There was a political mess that occurred behind the church scenes. It completely broke my heart. I was so invested in that little church. The details aren't important. I guess I thought that a small church wouldn't have that kind of ugly stuff going on. We ironed it out, but the taste of betrayal remained. Something delicate had wilted. We had found a new outlet for faith and worship, but our home church no longer felt like home.

Swinging a Dead Cat

A call came from Fort Myers. Fort Myers? (Ford and Edison used to hang out there.) I vaguely remembered the city from the touring days. That's the coastal Florida town where Way-FM started. It's infested with golf courses. A place where a fifty-year-old guy like me could start a youth group!

A new senior pastor wanted to fly us down. We'll call him Pastor Ed. The campus housed Westminster Presbyterian Church, Summit Christian School, and Hope Counseling Center. All ministries were staffed. The only empty position was the director of worship.

I asked Nate Larkin about possibly living in Florida. He enthused, "I think you and Lori might love it! They need worship leaders there. In Nashville, you can't swing a dead cat without hitting a worship leader!"

I appreciated the encouragement. But one thing troubled me: Why would you want to swing a dead cat?

We flew down to sultry Fort Myers on a couple of occasions. Lori and I prayed. God was knocking. And if you close the door on God, the Holy Spirit comes innuendo. They offered me the position. I hadn't had a full-time job in thirty years! I only knew how to be self-employed! The offer was about half of what we were making in the studio business. Plus, it was more expensive to live in Florida. Plus, housing was incredibly over-priced.

So, of course, we took it!

Songstory Writer Tip: Hymns are interesting things. These are songs that were made for voices to share. The best ones have rich theology. The Gettys are a great example of modern hymn writing. Have you ever tried it? Try using "teaching" lyrics. Some of my hymns have Christ's birth, death, and resurrection all included.

The church is fairly flooded with songs of "I Love You, Lord." I've written more of those than you can swing a dead cat at.

Now, such songs as "How Great the Father's Love" are a goalpost for me. If the Lord tarries, that song will work for the next hundred years. Try writing a song that will outlive you, and leave a legacy of Gospel truth. It's like trying to write a country song: simple music, deep lyrics. Sounds easy.

It isn't.

Songstory XXVIII

From Goose Creek to Blackbird Lane

*The problem with writing about religion is that
you run the risk of offending sincerely religious people,
and then they come after you with machetes.*
(Dave Barry)

*If you're going to go through hell anyway,
you might as well get a good song out of it.*
(Songstory)

A Dream Home for Someone Else

BY 2006, FRANKLIN, Tennessee, was giving us the Goodbye Look. The Thomas family had twenty years of stuff in our Goose Creek house (the goose was stuffed). The studio was crammed with two decades worth of tapes, guitars, mementos, and recording gear.

The barn housed two horses, three mowers, and a 1941 Ford 9N tractor. The garage was home to a red 1964 Ford Galaxie 500XL convertible. There were three more cars, a three-legged dog named Jake (sounds like a country song), cats named Moses and Elijah, and a partridge in a pear tree.

God was calling us to Fort Myers. We felt that we knew nearly everyone in Franklin. Lori and I started renovating the house for sale. Why did we do this? We let things get a little shabby, and we lived with it. But we dolled it up and made it into a dream home for someone else!

Crystal, Randall, and Sarah were at an age where they could stay or go. They opted to stay. Heart-wrenching. I made arrangements to drive a trailer full of equipment down on the first week of January, 2007. Lori stayed behind and sold or gave away stuff. One friend took a horse, a tractor, and the dog. The barn cats didn't relate to the human concept of ownership. They abandoned their new owner. The Galaxie (the "Butterfly Kisses" car) was sold to a stranger.

It was strange to pull out of the driveway and just say, "That's it." Abraham walked out of the rich culture of Chaldean Ur and wandered off into a foreign land. I was leaving Music City and headed to the bottom of the map, to the Peninsula of Retirement where they don't swing dead cats. Or if they did, they wouldn't hit a worship leader.

It felt like this was either a leap of faith or a step of stupidity. I pushed the car south, south, south until the asphalt ended. They say you're so far south, you're north again. The people down here hail from places like Ohio, Pennsylvania, or Wisconsin. You betcha.

I pulled into the church with a serious load of recording equipment and instruments. There to help me unload was Jim Lee. From that minute on, Jim became a dear brother to me. He would be the buddy who helped us with everything from Bible studies to dinner dances. God gave me a partner in the Gospel who couldn't write songs.

I rented a cozy little room on McGregor Boulevard near the Ford and Edison estates. The daily commute was lined with palm trees. The speed limit is 45, but the average Florida driver never exceeds 23. Which is good, because they can't see over the steering wheel.

The staff at Westminster Presbyterian included Dr. Vaughan Stanley. Vaughn's favorite band when he was a teenager was Iron Butterfly. I liked him immediately. The senior pastor, Ed, was an energetic man who had been an accountant. Alan was the youth pastor who had about forty kids, a stage, and a loud youth band. Cool. Mary Lou Capan was the head of Summit Christian School. Dr. Virginia Stewart was the head of Hope Counseling (who relocated to … wait for it … Franklin, Tennessee!).

The maintenance man was Mr. Tom. Mr. Tom was a non-recovering packrat. He often dressed in headband, wrist bands, knee socks, and shorts. All non-matching.

I could ask Tom, "Do you happen to have the stainless-steel side trim for a 1979 Mercedes 450SLC?"

And he would say, "Sure. Driver side or passenger?"

Once, a doctor had me swallow a camera to record the journey through my intestines. Tom asked, "When you're done with it, can I have it?"

"No, Tom. I'm not going searching for it, and neither are you."

Tom was downcast. "Seems like such a waste."

And Another Thing

Pastor Ed had sent me sermons the previous summer. The quality of his preaching was a factor in deciding to accept this call. I had sent him worship CDs. (These are silver things that spin.) I thought perhaps the quality of my music was a part of his decision. During the move, I wrote a worship song. I brought a guitar into Pastor Ed's office and played the new tune. He said, "I'm so glad to hear that you can sing!"

"You didn't listen to the CDs I sent you?"

"No! I only knew you wrote 'Butterfly Kisses'!"

This was strange. Fortunately, I could lead a band, direct a choir (nervously), and play guitar and other instruments. I had years of experience leading worship. Did no one read my résumé? Did no one research the guy they brought down from Nashville? I didn't take this as a good sign. It was the "Butterfly Kisses" curse in reverse.

I started creating a church music program from scratch. There had been no former organization to compare myself to. All of the dog-eared music seemed to be dated prior to 1985.

On the first day in the office, there was a new hitch. Pastor Ed said, "I don't like traditional music and choir. But the elders want you to lead a traditional service and organize a choir."

I hadn't sign up for this. "OK. I can do that."

After my first Sunday, we read through the blue prayer-request cards. One read, "My prayer request is that the worship leader and the pastor would wear a coat and tie." Really? I hadn't signed up for that, either. OK, I can do that. I was re-learning the politics of religion. No running in the hallways.

In the first month of leading worship, a tall, intimidating man in his eighties accosted me by the platform. He shook a hymnal at me and was yelling things like, "There are six hundred and twenty-eight hymns in this book! You didn't even play ONE of them!"

I forced my face into a beatific smile and waited for the tirade to end. I was counting on Proverbs 15:1, "A gentle answer turns away wrath." As he continued chewing me out, I noticed a man standing directly behind him, waiting in line.

The tall gentleman vented his entire spleen at me until he ran out of steam. I was prepared to respond with grace and humility. I wasn't allowed to answer. He stormed off, gathered his waiting family, and left.

I imagined the shorter man behind him stepping up and saying, "I'm really sorry that happened to you just now. Ignore him."

I was wrong. The shorter man said, "And another thing..." I don't even remember his complaint now. I only remember that it began with "And another thing..."

Blessed Subtraction

There was a dark-haired man in the church that organized a hymn sing in his home. A good number of white-haired people attended. This was presumably to offset the lack of good old songs in the Sunday service. Pastor Ed and I knew that we had a Q-tip mutiny on our hands. The dark-haired man systematically met with the pastors, then with me.

He said, "I'm representing a lot of people in this church. People are unhappy. So I'm here to help you." He looked around my office at record covers. "See, you play guitar. You play rock 'n' roll. But guitar is a folk instrument. Anything with strings is not a worship instrument." (My mind went to Psalm 33, 92, 149, 150, Isaiah 38, etc.) He continued, "That's why people are unhappy. The piano is a worship instrument, but not guitar." (Um, they both have strings.)

In this case, I was allowed to answer. I gave him my scriptural view of worship. The material was fresh in my mind since I had been through a lot of interviews. The dark-haired guy was not pleased. He wanted George Beverly Shea. He called my style heavy metal.

So the dark-haired man stirred up a contingent of older people to leave the church. Romans 16 says to mark such a man who causes division. I think he was able to make about a hundred people unhappy, but only a few actually left with him. He's a deacon at a sister church now. If they are singing "How Great Thou Art," perhaps he is happy.

I re-wrote some hymn lyrics for people like the dark-haired man (sung to the tune of "Blessed Assurance"):

Blessed subtraction; glad you are gone!
You kept complaining all the day long:
"I miss the organ! I hate the drums!"

All you contribute is flapping your gums!
This is your story, this is your song;
threatened to leave us all season long—
This is your story, this is your song;
blessed subtraction, glad you are gone!

The problem in Florida is that you have retired people who think, "I've done my time. I'm not serving anymore. It's time for others to serve me." Scripture teaches otherwise. There is a high priority on serving, and there is no biblical mandate for retiring from a life of serving. "For even the Son of Man did not come to be served, but to serve, and to give his life as a ransom for many" (Mark 10:45).

There were many wonderful worshippers at Westminster, and many showed appreciation for our music. But there was a noticeable deficit of love. And love is a major earmark of Christ's disciples: "By this all people will know that you are my disciples, if you have love for one another" (John 13:35). After services on Sunday, I often locked up. There was no invitation to lunch for the unpopular new music guy.

Before Lori was able to finish selling the Goose Creek house, I was very much alone on this job. People wanted music from the 1800s or the 1980s. Nothing new. I thought we had fought the worship wars in the '70s. And I thought we had won. Westminster had been in a retired bubble that kept young people out. They ignored the Jesus Movement. The word "change" was anathema.

With Christ as my rock, and Lori as my wife, I determined to outlast the culture of resistance.

Rotten Eggs

Once Lori arrived in Fort Myers, we got to house hunting. In Tennessee, we had had the ultimate hilltop gingerbread ranch house. Now, we prayed for a house that exemplified the Floridian lifestyle. We prayed for a house with a pool overlooking a lake. We found it on Blackbird Lane. My lawn-mowing skills (a matter of being able to find your car in Tennessee) were no longer needed. They have lawn-mowing services. We had sprinklers now.

The only problem with the local sprinklers is when people use well water. It stinks! So people set their lawn systems for 4 A.M. The whole neighborhood smells like rotten eggs. I thought Lori knew this. We had a revelation one afternoon while walking the neighborhood. We passed a house where they were testing the sprinkler system.

Lori slapped my arm, "Did you fart?"

I was a little hurt. "What? That's not me! That's the smell of well water!"

Lori said, "No, it's not. I know that smell. Ever since we moved here, you start farting at four in the morning and the stink wakes me up."

I stopped walking. "That's when the neighbor's sprinklers go on."

A light went on and her eyes got wide like eggs over easy. "Oh. Hahahahaha! I thought it was something in the Florida food! Hahahaha!"

I would have been offended if I hadn't been laughing so hard.

God Has His Reasons

At the end of my first year of worship wars, Pastor Ed shook my hand. "Congratulations! You're the first worship director who has ever lasted one entire year!" Hm. What did all the other worship leaders know that I didn't?

Jeff Taylor was the general manager at Way-FM. He was an ALLIES fan. During a lunch, he asked, "Why did you come to Westminster?"

I asked, "Why do you ask?"

Jeff said, "It's pretty much known as a church for retired people. It just doesn't seem to fit with Randy Thomas from ALLIES." He suggested some mega churches that he thought would fit my talents better. He offered to find me a cooler job.

I was a round peg in a square hole. But, for some reason, I insisted, "God brought us to Westminster. He has His reasons."

In our second year at Westminster, the "weird" started to get worse. There was the financial crisis that made the real estate bubble burst. Lori and I had put a lot of money into our house. That money vaporized over-night. There were other storm clouds gathering.

Pastor Ed, being an accountant, could see that finances were going to be tight, so he worked out a secret plan. He had the elders read a book called *Good to Great* that taught about getting the right people on your bus and the wrong people off. What the church didn't know was that Pastor Ed was planning to throw his whole staff under the bus!

In a long series of events, the staff got picked off, one by one. To pull this off, Pastor Ed exhibited a pattern of stretching the truth beyond reason. I was offered half salary. Because of the lies and intrigue, I asked for severance. It was likely that Lori and I were going to lose big time on our failed relocation to Florida. The elders didn't want to let us go. This curdled Pastor Ed's "Good to Great" idea. I wasn't happy about continuing to work with a narcissist. Then Pastor Ed got busted by the elders: They caught him in a blatant lie.

Pastor Ed concocted another web of lies as he was counseled in a multi-church effort to restore his ministry. The Presbytery had to get Pastor Ed off their bus. Guess who was left on staff?

The unpopular guitar slinger who chafed in a suit and tie.

The church suffered the expected contractions. Some people left because they felt Pastor Ed was treated unfairly. Such irony. In the ensuing mess, Jim and Terri Lee helped hold down what was left of the fort with Lori and me. We knew if we could make it through the summer of 2009 and keep the doors open, we could make it through anything.

By God's grace, we made it. The Lord gives and the Lord takes away. Blessed be the name of the Lord (Job 1:21).

Continuing on partial salary and the church taking up both of our schedules took its toll. Lori and I went into debt. After things got better, the church went on a hiring spree. They started hiring missing staff while Lori and I were in a financial hole. Faithful Jim Lee went to the elders and asked for my salary to be restored. Finally, it was.

Lori and I had suffered several lean years, but the church recovered. I guess God had His reasons to keep us on the bus.

Songstory Writer Tip: Use your dark times to write what may be your best songs. They say there is a purpose for pain: fruit grows in the valley, and all that. The suffering artist cliché does not need to be taken too seriously. Don't cut off your ear like a Dutch post-impressionist, but let the lessons that are coming at you come out in the music.

For some reason, singing the blues can be a happy experience. It's cathartic. And singing a sweet song (even "Butterfly Kisses") can feel wrong* at times. Performers

---

* When does singing "Butterfly Kisses" feel wrong? There are rare occasions when people are drinking and dancing (which is not the problem—unless they are Baptists), and I will be asked to sing That Song. If it seems to be the wrong time or the wrong place, I'll sing "Mustang Sally" instead.

have to sing a song often under the guise of "the show must go on." But the writer can bring something up from the heart that can transmit pleasure or pain or a mixture of the two.

It's a powerful thing. You've probably felt it from other people's songs—and that is what you aspire to. It's not easy. Listen to some Bryan Duncan, the master of the autobiographical. His life comes out in songs. If you're going to go through hell anyway, you might as well get a good song out of it.

Songstory XXIX

Nashville Music Garden

To those of you who received honors,
awards and distinctions, I say well done.
And to the C students, I say you, too,
can be president of the United States.
(George W. Bush)

Whatever you ask in my name, this I will do,
that the Father may be glorified in the Son.
(John 14:13)

ON SEPTEMBER 29, 2009, the Nashville Hall of Fame
unveiled their Nashville Music Garden, "Walk Through
the Roses." They awarded a bloom to legendary artists
and outstanding songs, including "Butterfly Kisses." I
flew up to Nashville from our Florida paradise. Bob flew
in from his Vegas oasis. It promised to be a cool time of
seeing many of our Nashville buddies.

I hadn't seen Bob for years. He was as hilarious as
ever. We hugged and took photos. Many of the honorees
were either living legends like little Jimmie Dickens
or family members of departed stars. They did it up
Nashville-style. We sat outside on wooden chairs with
the Country Music Hall of Fame as a backdrop.

There were some serendipitous moments before the
presentation. The man seated in front of me said hello

and asked where I was from. It felt odd to say, "Florida." Nashville used to be my home. He was from Kentucky. I said, "It's such an honor to see the 'Butterfly Kisses' flower placed on an honoree list with such legendary songs as the 'Tennessee Waltz'!"

He said, "I'm glad you feel that way! My father, Redd Stewart, wrote that song!"

The lady sitting next to me introduced herself as Jett. Unusual name. After introducing myself, I said, "I hear that some of Hank Senior's family will be here. I'm glad that Nashville remembers what a towering influence Hank was. He was the Original, to me. Hank Williams started all this!"

Jett teared up a little. "Thanks for saying that. He was my daddy!"

I'd almost forgotten what a down-home world Nashville could be. Lovable Ralph Emory emceed the event. Lynn Anderson and Barbara Mandrell co-hosted. Barbara had a quotable quip. She said, "Did you notice that my flower is understated and petite, while Dolly Parton's rose is ostentatious—with huge blooms?"

The after party was Nashville casual. Marty Raybon of Shenandoah fame remembered my name, which surprised me. (He is a brother in Christ. He also may have that pastor gene for remembering people's names.) The legendary Patty Page was all grins. Bob was excited to take a photo with her!

My lovely daughter Crystal was able to join us for the dinner. I was proud to brag on Crystal's talent and music. I even shamelessly handed out some of her music!

When interviewed by the media, I said something like, "Most award shows celebrate artists *or* songwriters. Only Nashville could create a music garden that honors BOTH the artists AND the songs. It's certainly a high honor to see our 'Butterfly Kisses' bloom in the company of such unforgettable songs and legendary artists."

Barbara Mandrell interrupted our dinner salad with a prayer of thanksgiving to "Our Heavenly Father" for the lovely day. She ended the prayer most definitely in JESUS' name. Nashville still has some Gospel salt and light left in it. The day reminded me of a song that Bill Sprouse Jr. wrote in the '70s: "God loves country music; an angel told me so."

Bob and I took photos with the "Butterfly Kisses" bloom. It's a dainty yellow flower. Unlike a compact rose, this bloom looks a bit like delicate butterfly wings. Check out the company that "Butterfly Kisses" is in: "Amazing Grace," Amy Grant, "Blue Suede Shoes," "Coal Miner's Daughter," "Coat of Many Colors," Elvis, Kitty Wells, LeAnn Rimes, Lee Greenwood's "American Patriot," Little Jimmy Dickens, Lynn Anderson, Minnie Pearl, Patsy Cline, "Pretty Woman," "Purple Haze," Reba McEntire, "Ring of Fire," "Rocky Top," Shania Twain, "Sweet Dreams," "Sweet Home Alabama," "Tennessee Waltz," and many more! As Reba would say, "Dern!"

SOL in Franklin

That evening I joined Bob, Reggie Hamm, Dennis Patton, and some other buddies at a noisy Franklin restaurant called SOL. I had some weird seafood enchiladas. Perhaps it was a dare. (You can always count on fresh seafood in Tennessee...)

Bob admitted it was his fifty-fourth birthday. BIRTHDAY? I spied waitresses sneaking into the bar with a candle and cupcake on a platter. Figured Dennis or someone had made arrangements to surprise Bob with a cupcake. Sweet. We started singing, "Happy Birthday to You." Everyone in the bar joined in. (You know how these things go.) "Happy birthday to you" continued.

The waiters paraded toward us singing. Then they filed right by us and kept going to a table in the back. The song died and ended with, "Happy Birthday dear.............."

Silence.

Bob threw up his hands and announced, "Story of my life!" Then he jokingly commented to the dispersing waiters, "You shouldn't have!"

Reggie chimed in, "No! You *should* have!"

After dinner, we gathered under a streetlight on Main and watched the hipster nightlife. It was a reunion of ALLIES gig stories and general music business reminiscing by the jaded fortunate few. Bob treated me to a cigar. I shouldn't have. For me, a cigar is more of a curse than a blessing. We lit up. I turned green.

Was it the seafood enchiladas? Was it the cigar? Something just didn't sit right with me. I didn't want to spew in front of all my buddies on such a great night. But there was that queasy feeling. Then my mouth watered. *Oh, please. Not tonight.* Then an involuntary heave. Then *Vesuvius eruptus.*

In quiet desperation, I bent over a storm drain area. (It was too late to run into SOL, and I was wearing shoes that I wanted to keep.) The "seafood" reappeared, worse for wear.

I imagined people driving by thinking, "Is that the guy from ALLIES? Throwing up in the gutter in front of a bar? Serves him right for trying to take credit for Bob's song..." Maybe this is why they named the place SOL.

My Christian fellows shuffled their feet and pretended not to notice. Always a sweetheart, Bob fetched a soda water for me. But that wasn't the capper for the evening. The waitress came out and presented Bob with a bill. Like a surprise parting gift for Bob's birthday, Dennis had gone home without paying for his meal.

Bob paid it.

Songstory Writer Tip: Use what I call the "Change the Meaning of the Chorus" trick. Let's say you have a chorus to a song called "Blue Skies over Montana." Verse one talks about a little boy who dreams of being a cowboy who sleeps under the stars. When a cowboy opens his eyes in the morning, what does he see? Blue Skies over Montana! Then (verse two), as a young man, our hero tries to ride a crazy old bull named El Diablo. But the bull throws him hat over heels high into the air, and what does he see? Blue Skies over Montana! In verse three, the old cowboy dies. They bury him out on the range. And where is the cowboy now? He's out there sleeping under those Blue Skies over Montana!

See what I did there? You stayed with me because I told a story *and* the chorus took on a slightly different meaning each time. That's good songwriting.

Songstory XXX

Jeremiah Is a Bullfrog!

If I only had a dollar for every song I've sung...
(John Fogarty)

We used to play until the police shut us down.
Now we party 'til the paramedics roll in.
(Songstory)

AT WESTMINSTER, I picked up some new musical skills doing choir and hymns. But some of my older skills were going unused. Was there a horn band in Fort Myers? A trumpet player hipped me to a local band called Alter Ego. Some of the members were lawyers and doctors. Thus the name. I showed up with a guitar and amp one night and faked my way through three hours of classic rock songs with them. From then on, I was in.

Alter Ego plays some regular dance club spots and an occasional corporate gig, wearing tuxedos. I was fortunate to play original songs when I was young. Now, I'm fortunate to play covers. (I'm not old. I'm a *legacy* act.)

The bar world can be a rough life for young musicians. Having a day job in a church and casual night gigging is a manageable deal. Lori is supportive, and our local dance crowd is retirees. We don't have to watch out for bar fights. We watch out for dance floor injuries: "I got down; now I can't get up!" We used to play until the police shut us down. Now we party 'til the paramedics roll in.

Lori and I started a band called Highway 41, named after the road that runs from Michigan all the way through to Miami. Our first engagement was a high-profile country club. I hired a huge sound system. When the band showed up, the system was supposed to be set up outside, ready to go. But the sound man had the flu. He was nearly comatose. It was time to start, and there was no sound. The lady promoter was so distressed, she went home!

We turned monitors around and played blind in an effort just to get things going. I guess the people at this particular club were used to a particular oldies song list. As we were playing "I Heard It Through the Grapevine," a club member came and stood beside me. He looked like the grumpy old Muppet character: bald head, constant frown, folded arms. We had a conversation as I kept playing and singing. He stood to my right, staring into my ear.

I said, "Can I help you?"

"CREEDENCE!"

"Sorry?"

"DON'T YOU KNOW CREEDENCE?"

"Sure. What song would you like?"

"JEREMIAH IS A BULLFROG!"

I had to sing some backing vocals while he stared at my head. As I backed away from the mic, I suggested, "Perhaps you mean 'Joy to the World' by Three Dog

Night." (The opening line of which is Jeremiah *was* a bullfrog, but I didn't have time to argue the tense.)

He yelled again: "CREEDENCE! JEREMIAH IS A BULLFROG!"

"Okay, but I think you're referring to a Hoyt Axton song made famous by Three Dog Night!"

He stared at the side of my face, furrowing his brow for a while, while I played. Then he yelled, "YOU'RE *WRONG!*" And he left.

It was rough trying to start up our own band (what with Muppet hecklers). We went back to sitting in with Alter Ego. Drummer Todd Caruso suggested that Lori and I could do well as a duo. Why didn't I think of that? We scheduled a lunch with local entertainers (and believers) Billy Dean and Dawn. They graciously explained the country club scene to us.

Having had my posterior kicked when starting new ventures, I asked Billy, "How long do you think it will take to get our weekend calendar filled with quality clubs?"

He said, "There's a lot of work out there. You guys should be up and running in the first year!" I was dubious.

Billy was right. In 2015, we launched Randy and Lori as a duo (randyandlori.com). We were fairly busy, and in 2016, we hit full stride. On the average gig, an affluent bunch is seated and waited upon as we play "music to be ignored by." We'll end our dinner set with something like "All I Ask of You." Lori's voice usually wows even the least interested diner.

After a break, we come back with a dance set. Thanks to the average age of our crowds, they begin to tire out between 8:30 and 9:00. The later set depends upon how much energy is left in the room. We have been bribed to play for five hours straight. (That's rare.) We have also had club staff send us home early. (Early being 8:30.)

That's our new sideline. This is beyond leading worship at two churches and the occasional out-of-town worship. I'll occasionally sit in with some buddies jamming around seaside haunts. Once in a while, Randy and Lori are asked to "perform" for an event. This can be anything from a private Christmas party to a large corporate fundraiser.

The Heights Foundation is our favorite local cause. We have done events with Cliff Williams* (bassist with AC/DC) or with Billy Dean (of "Billy the Kid" fame) or with the Heights Party Band—which is an excuse to play whatever songs the band wants to play. Randy and Lori are booked up to eighteen months in advance. That makes me wonder how old I will be when I hang it up. George Burns was asked if he expected to live to be a hundred. George gestured with his cigar and winked, "I've got to … I'm *booked!*"

We rarely do "Butterfly Kisses." Friends advise us to play it more often and to self-promote. If we're doing a dinner/dance, it doesn't fit to me. There are musicians who have innate marketing skills to turn a little bit of success into a major career boost. I seem to have a gift for

---

* After hearing Lori sing, Cliff said to her, "You're a mother f- - --r of a singer!" It gave Lori pause. She'd never heard a compliment worded that way before.

She responded, "Um..........................thank you??"

keeping my past career a secret. When people request the Dolly song, I get Lori to sing it.

When Lori sings, I know I've found my true musical home. The Randy and Lori thing is so real. The honeymoon continues after thirty-five years! I get to play a more supportive role, which is where I excel.

Lori does an amazing job of singing multiple styles well. She's world-class. Often, after a gig, local fans will come up to us and say (looking at Lori), "Oh, your voice is just spectacular! Just fabulous! You are amazing!"

And then they look at me and say, "Oh. Um. And you were good, too...."

Songstory Writer Tip: Do you have a song that needs a long explanation? This is probably a sign that you need to improve it. Probably by throwing it out. Let's say you have a good song that has an odd backstory. My advice is to play it without introduction to a group of people. A good song will prompt someone to say, "What was the story behind your song?" See what just happened? You have upgraded your act from amateur apologies to a thoughtful songwriter interview.

I've heard a million song introductions. You know how many I remember? *None.* But I do remember one great writer (Phil Madiera) sitting down with an old guitar. He looked ruffled. The guy's face told a story. He was about to play for a group of people who were ignoring him. With zero explanation, he began playing a great song. I was spellbound. The song just took command of the room. (Sure, there were a few musically deaf people who missed it and kept talking. Their loss.)

A great song doesn't strut or have an ego. It has a presence that can't be denied.

Songstory XXXI

Tag: Ten Things You Can Glean from Songstory

Wisdom cries aloud in the street,
in the markets she raises her voice;
at the head of the noisy streets she cries out;
at the entrance of the city gates she speaks:
"How long, O simple ones, will you love being simple?
How long will scoffers delight in their scoffing
and fools hate knowledge?
If you turn at my reproof, behold,
I will pour out my spirit to you;
I will make my words known to you."
(Proverbs 1:20–23)

I ONCE GAVE a presentation at a songwriter class. I had already heard some of their songs, so I knew there was a crying need for improvement. It didn't go well. The amateur songwriters didn't like my advice. They didn't like it one bit. I talked about re-writing and striving for excellence. Apparently, this bunch felt that their songs could use no improvement. Rather than asking questions, many of them argued with me.

One guy with white hair had listened. He took notes. One guy. The note-taking guy raised his hand. I said, "Yes?"

The note-taking guy stood up. He faced the amateur songwriters behind him. He said, "I don't have a question. I've learned a lot today. The thing I don't understand is all you people that are arguing with Randy. I'm just curious—how many of you have won a Grammy?" He sat down.

That was nice of him. They still didn't listen.

Wisdom cries out in the streets. Now we come to the part of the book that is like the practical application of a sermon. This is my attempt to boil my life journey down to Ten Life Lessons. Consider this the Takeaway—what you can learn from Songstory.

Takeaway 1. Learn to do one thing very well. In my case, it was playing guitar. If you do something badly, what would it take for you to do it well? (Probably a commitment of time and an application of discipline.) There's no way around preparation. Study and practice precede excellence. If someone reads this book and ups his or her game at playing an instrument or writing songs or selling real estate, it will have all been worth it.

Learning to do one thing well leads to other things! For me, playing guitar led to songwriting, which led to record producing, which led to engineering, which all led to a career, which led to a Grammy, which led to a book. (For some reason, in my head I'm singing, *"I don't know why she swallowed a fly; perhaps she'll die."*)

Takeaway 2. Learn how to turn what you love into what you do. The old adage "Choose a job you love, and you will never have to work a day in your life" applies here. (That quote is attributed to Mark Twain and Confucius.

I'm going with Confucius.) The idea that you will never work is patently untrue. But if you are going to spend fifty years doing something, it better not be something you hate!

Socrates said, "To do is to be." Sartre said, "To be is to do." Sinatra said, "Do be do be do." But all seriousness aside, you should wake up and smell the roses along the way. Your identity and your proclivities need to have a meet and greet. Elvis started as a truck driver. Good thing he switched to hip swiveling. What is it that you do? What is it that you love? I identify as a Christian musician. It's what I *be*. Those are two identifying terms for how God made me. Can you identify the real you in two words? Try it. Then it's just a matter of turning the "what you be" into "what you *do*."

Some people have a day job that makes money and a weekend hobby that loses money. This is where I challenge you not to be amateurs who revel in mediocrity. You're going to have to create some mighty good art before someone is going to buy it. Now, if you fail to monetize the thing you love, you can still win. Lots of professionals are very happy losing a little money to do their side gig. Pay to play.

I'm just saying your art should be like your character: Don't stop improving.

Takeaway 3. Seek out associates and mentors who excel at what you want to do. I'm using general terms here. For my Songstory life, seeking out associates means getting a band together. For you, it may be Bible college or woodshop.

Ask and ye shall receive. You'd be surprised how many wise people give out advice. Wisdom cries aloud in the street. Hunt down somebody who loves what you love.

I remember standing with Michael Hodge when he met an aging jazz guitar legend. Mike said, "How can I get lessons from you? Do you have an agency?" Michael was assuming such a famous and accomplished player would have handlers.

The old master looked up, handed Michael a card, and said, "Just call me. We can start tomorrow."

What worked for me was learning to play with a garage band. Then we graduated to a high school dance band. My advice is—keep graduating. Don't repeat first grade if you don't have to.

Takeaway 4. Join a cause. Your cause may be world peace. (Good luck with that. Have fun singing at the pageant!) It always helps to be a part of something big. It gives you mission. This is the stuff that can carry you through a lifetime.

Christianity is the greatest unfailing cause (no matter what John Lennon said). The gates of hell will not prevail against the church of Christ (Matthew 16:17–19). People are saying that the American church is in decline.

Fear not, neither let your heart be afraid. The church will never fail. We may be forced underground. They may feed us to the lions. But you will never, ever, ever stop us. We are God's people. Take Gamaliel's advice from Acts chapter 5. It's no use taking up a cause against God.

Maybe you have benefitted from a twelve-step program. Perhaps you are a vet or a cancer survivor. Whatever has impacted your life is probably your cause.

Takeaway 5. God, family, and marriage are more important than business and career. If you are an atheist, you can remove God from the top of the list and say, "Bah humbug." It's still better than serving mammon. Atheists sometimes behave like Christians should and Christians sometimes behave like fools. If you prioritize the right things, God seems to bless wisdom—no matter who you are.

I've witnessed artists and songwriters who spent more time and energy on their careers than on their families. This always ends badly. Children should never be treated as unwanted beings. When children have their lives torn apart, it is usually over bad decisions or money.

Wisdom cries out in the street.

Takeaway 6. Practice perpetual forgiveness. There is an old proverb that says, "Holding a grudge is like taking poison and expecting it to kill your enemy." Any partnership between sinners is bound to fall into misunderstandings and hurt feelings. We're all sinners (Romans 3:23). Any marriage, any church, any band, and any business will need a fresh supply of forgiveness.

Don't drink the poison. There is a frightening biblical mandate: We must forgive if we wish to be forgiven (Matthew 6:15). The most-ignored scripture in the Bible is in Matthew 18. Jesus said to go to your brother if there is an issue. What do we do? We always talk behind our brother's (or sister's) back. We only confront him or her as a last resort. People actually *die* before settling accounts with family and friends.

Talk to your father, your mother, your brother, your sister, or your estranged friend before it's too late. On rare occasions, the offended party may say, "Screw you." At least you tried. In a great majority of cases, just reaching out may mend the wound.

There is unspeakable joy in forgiveness.

Takeaway 7. When you come to a fork in the road, take it. Yogi Berra said this. Of course, he lived at the far end of a lane that went in a loop. What I mean is, when you come to the end of something, create a new path. When you ask wise elderly people for advice on life, they all say, "Keep going. Keep growing."

Wisdom cries out in the streets. Take a lesson from Winston Churchill who said, "This is the lesson: never give in, never give in, never, never, never, never—in nothing, great or small, large or petty—never give in except to convictions of honour and good sense. Never yield to force; never yield to the apparently overwhelming might of the enemy."

Life is littered with dead ends. You may even come to the end of yourself. You will learn the pain of starting over. But, it is the pain of New Life. Reinvent yourself. Start a new career. Learn to love again. Learn to trust again.

I like the lines in the movie *A League of Their Own*. The baseball manager asks his player why she is going to quit. She says, "It got too hard."

He responds, "It's supposed to be hard. If it wasn't hard, everyone would do it. The 'hard' is what makes it *great!*"

Takeaway 8. Take lessons when you are younger. Give lessons when you are older. Don't be like me; I never took guitar lessons. I learned the hard way. Don't be the guitar player who turns his back so that other guitar players can't see what he's doing. If someone learns from you, it doesn't take anything away from you.

Soak up stuff from a mentor. I learned from listening to B.B. King, Eric Clapton, and Larry Carlton. YouTube can enable you to learn from the best of the best. Take it in, and make it your own. Then the day will come when someone asks you for a lesson. Give it away freely (Matthew 10:5–8).

One of the greatest moments of my life was when I was approached in a music store on Broadway in Nashville. A young guitarist asked me about a specific solo I had played back in 1979 or so. I said, "I'm sorry. I really don't remember it." He sat me down and showed me my solo. He showed me *my solo!* Note for note.

Recently, I made a guitar video lesson for my nephews. I heard from their mom that they watched it multiple times. That's a win. Whatever hard-earned wisdom you learned when you were young, give it out when you get older. Mentor someone. It's a win-win.

Takeaway 9. Lighten up. Have fun along the way. I hope you have laughed at many of my stories. I could never have a career as a funeral director. Laughing with family and friends is just about the greatest thing in life. I do it a lot. I've read about ten thousand books in my life. I mainly remember the ones that made me laugh.

Fun is doing what you love, and loving what you do. Whatever you do, if you mix in a little fun, you can be great. Wag more. Bark less.

Takeaway 10. Be an adult learner. Keep putting things in your brain. What the dormouse said; feed your head (Grace Slick lyric). When you stop growing, you start getting smaller. Read books. Try new things. Stretch your mind. My musical growth spurts started in my twenties and lasted through my forties. I didn't really learn theology until I was in my late forties. I became a worship director in my fifties. I started writing books in my sixties.

Beware of thinking you know all you need to know. This will stunt your brain. Have you known people who didn't learn how to use computers? Perhaps you've known people who got stuck in a time-warp; the world moved on, but they haven't. (People who write books about what they did in the '70s and '80s…)

I once saw a map that was found inside the staircase of an antebellum house in Franklin, Tennessee. The map was suitable for framing. It showed what the historic town was like in 1870. It was accurate. But imagine if you used that map to get around Franklin in 2021. It's not going to work.

Wisdom calls out in the streets.

Keep revising your map.

࿇

Songstory Writer Tip: In any field of endeavor, networking yields major benefits. You want to get your songs recorded? It will not happen without a network. Don't have a network? Create one, if you have to. Connecting with a co-writer, or a producer, or an artist is how things happen. Carpe that Diem!

Nashville is the ultimum* network. L.A. is much more spread out. New York is tough to break into. Austin is on the rise. Hits come out of Miami, Chicago, and other hotbeds. Even here in little Fort Myers, there is a songwriter's association. I know it can be like the first day in grade school. It's tough breaking into a new social circle.

I've never heard of a hit where a writer wrote a song, showed it to no one, and Taylor Swift tracked him down and begged for a chance to record it.

Even Christian songwriters find out that when miracles happen, God uses *people*. Amen.

---

* Ultimum is a word I just invented. Just now. It's a combination of optimum and ultimate. Work with me.

Songstory XXXI.V (31.5)

So, You Wanna Join the Christian Club?

We all have crosses to bear,
and we are all trying on different ones for a good fit.
(Vasily Zhukovsky)

SO, YOU WANNA join the Christian club? If I were a salesman, I would point out the best features: ETERNAL LIFE! GOD'S FAVOR! LOVE! PEACE! JOY! Heaven and forgiveness are major selling points. You can't beat the Christian Brochure! The retirement benefits are to die for! So why isn't everybody signing up? Probably because we all suspect there is something in the fine print. And it's probably in Leviticus somewhere between goats dying and blood being sprinkled!

I'm willing to be the honest, bumbling guy who shows you the factory invoice. Have a seat in my show-room office. Let's examine the features that are not on the window sticker of the vehicle. Brace yourself. (Imagine me touching the tips of my fingers while I run these down…)

There's a cost to be counted. God will change your life. You're required to join a club (the Church). There are dues … (whispering) *although I'm told the average*

Christian gives 4 percent of his income, so it's easy to be above average in this category.

There's a Christian-ese way of talking. (I just felt led to share that.)

Prepare yourself for disappointment. I mean, have you *met* me? Hey, even John the Baptist was disappointed in JESUS (Luke 7:19)! Don't get me wrong—Jesus is our Perfect Righteousness (1 Peter 2:22). But Christians will invariably disappoint you. I'm certain that some already have.

The draft board is unpredictable. If you want to volunteer, you can't (John 14:6). If you don't want to volunteer, God may enlist you anyway (John 15:16). Go ask the Apostle Paul. And Jesus said, "I am the true vine" (John 15:1). Vines are invasive.

So don't trust a preacher's pitch if he assures you that your life would be better if you just added in some Jesus. The Lord is not a supplement. He will insist on being your first love beyond all else. Think about the end-game: Heaven is a God-centered realm of constant worship. (The herd just thinned.)

That's why I respect happy atheists. They have looked under the hood of religion and decided, "SCREW THIS!" Agnostics reserve the right to not adhere to their own personal non-religion.

Let's get real: 90 percent of Christians struggle with wanting the benefits of Christendom, while wanting to be Lord of their own lives. The other 10 percent are liars. Plus, if you're a Christian, and this rant offends you, God says you have to forgive me (Matthew 18:35)!

So, full disclosure: You would be joining a club of broken losers who keep injuring themselves.

After forty-nine years of faith, I see the following as non-negotiable: You trust Christ as Savior. You believe His Word. The Holy Spirit changes you. God owns you.

If all that didn't scare you off—let's face the *real* danger and sign you up for nursery duty!

Songstory Writer Tip: Learn about chord substitutions. When you sing a C, you can play a C-major chord. You can also try an A-minor. Or F. Substituting a G-sharp can be your "surprise chord." What's a surprise chord? Listen to the A-major chord in "Something in the Way She Moves." Classic bait and switch. In "Change the World" (co-written by my good buddy Gordon Kennedy), you have the G-sharp used as an unusual transition to the chorus. Clapton used a surprise C-sharp minor when going from chorus to verse on "Layla." This may even be why "Change the World" caught his ear.

Surprise chords work well in your bridge. Let's say you have a song that drones somewhat in the key of E. Write a bridge in the key of G. Your ears will say, "Thank you." See? It might help keep your listeners interested in your song.

CODA

If You Know How Many Guitars You Have, You Don't Have Enough

It's just a piece of wood with wires attached to it. (John Lennon, referring to his black Beatles-era Rickenbacker)

GRETSCH DELIVERED A new guitar to the studio for Chet Adkins. Chet put it through the paces. A young engineer marveled, saying, "That's the greatest sounding guitar I ever heard!" Then he said, "Those Gretsches are the best! Just listen to that Gretsch!"

Chet smiled. He put the guitar on a stand and then went and stood beside the young guy. They both admired the new instrument, gleaming under the lights. Just when the silence got to be a little uncomfortable, Chet pointed to the Gretsch and asked the engineer, "How's it sound now?"

People ask me, "How many guitars do you have? You know you can play only one at a time..."

It's usually women who ask that. So I think it's a good idea to answer, "How many pairs of shoes do you have? You know you can only wear one pair at a time..." The truth is, I don't know how many guitars I have. I have a theory that more is more. And the best guitars come *looking* for you.

In Odessa, Texas, I met a guy who said, "I'll trade you an old 1959 Fender Stratocaster for that new 1978 Les Paul." Had to follow up on that.

Well, he had a stark raving *naked* 1961 Strat! Someone had stripped the finish, presumably because of the love-it-or-hate-it sea-foam green. He wanted the new Les Paul. "OK. Deal." Michael McGuire and Wayne Charvel restored it. You hear it on "In My Life" by ALLIES and on "Julianna Wilson" by Identical Strangers.

A tawny 1973 Fender Jazz bass looked me up. Joel Madden's '71 bass had been stolen. The '73 was panic-purchased to play for a weekend. Joel heard about a guy playing his bass in a San Bernardino nightclub. Joel took that bass out of the thief's hands while he was performing! He took his bass home. His wife asked, "What are you going to do with the new bass you bought? You can only play one at a time!" The new one was sold to me the next morning.

A chocolate 1971 Gibson ES335 came looking for me from a band called Whalin' Jonah. It was 500 bucks, if memory serves. You can see that on YouTube, and it saw a lot of studio action. The '71 paired well with a special-order Mesa Boogie Mark 2 amp. There was a Caribou Ranch SCB session with Richie Furay (Buffalo Springfield), where Richie played the first half of a solo on "Carry Me." I played the second section on the brown '71 through the Boogie. United Airlines later pulverized that instrument. Phil Keaggy was my witness to the carnage.

I have a thing for 1968 Les Pauls. Someone told me that they were made from wood left in storage from 1958. I had two '68 Les Pauls and a red '68 ES335. Had. (Sniff!)

Maybe the best guitar amps are the ones you go looking for. A bunch of us learned to love a squatty little I-can't-believe-how-heavy-that-is amp called the Ampeg VT 40. Mine was purchased at Lopez' Music House, San Bernardino.

Mr. Lopez bought the building that was the original McDonalds brother's hamburger stand at 14th and E Street. It has been erased from McDonald's history. My homies and I have memories of the original old sign being "repurposed" to read The Music House. History books say they tore it down in 1972 and rebuilt in 1980. Funny … all my friends remember drooling on music equipment there between 1970 and 1975.

That Ampeg amp was carted in a case purchased from Bob Carlisle. It was stenciled "Fragile B. Carlisle," which Greg Eckler fondly pronounced as "Fra-GEE-lay, bee car-LIZ-ley." The case was resold to Bob, along with the amp. By this time I had fitted the amp with weighty Altec speakers, bringing the heft of amp and case to well over 100 pounds! Bob used to cart it in the bed of his Chevy truck.

When locking up his truck, Bob would have to lift that booger out of the bed and muscle it up onto the bench seat. Sometime around 1980, Bob parked in front of a Mexican restaurant. The road cased amplifier was so hefty that Bob said (of potential thieves), "If they can LIFT it; they can HAVE it!"

They did; and they do.

Michael McGuire of Valley Arts built me the Stratovarious. It is serial #000077. It's a hand-built cherry sunburst HSH quilted maple body with Birdseye maple neck. Expensive, but worth it. On its first day, our sound man dropped it. On asphalt. It bears scars. This was a major player on SCB and all ALLIES records. "Habit Of Hate" and "Mule-Headed Man" were examples of my more frenetic solos on the Stratovarious.

Jim Kelly amps are heard on anything I did between 1980 and 1993. Jim made three of them for me. Custom; expensive. Two of my Kellys went to studio ace Jerry McPherson in Nashville. The last holdout was a very special koa wood combo that was sold to a mysterious buyer through a broker. The buyer turned out to be ... Joe Bonamassa!

During the '90s, ESP built me a bunch of good instruments. I favored a tobacco sunburst Strat called Toby.

Wait, what about acoustics? I used a black Gibson Dove for a long time. I traded it, along with a really wild Charvel guitar, for a 1983 Martin HD28. Stunning sound. This was my Shania guitar. Bill Martin of Reverse Tension Guitars sent me a handmade beauty that is my new favorite. I also use two of Bill's RT guitars live. I like the initials.

One night a Gibson ES333 came looking for me. A no-nonsense workhorse. It was purchased out of the trunk of an old car on a rainy night from a guy known as The Duckman!

My wife asked, "What are we doing in a dark parking lot behind Lowe's with a bunch of cash?"

I assured her with, "I'm buying a guitar. Cash. From the Duck. This is going to make a great story!"

A 1968 Gibson ES335 looked me up. On the internet. We call it Stories. It has scars that indicate it has seen a lot of action. (If that thing could only talk.)

Then a 2017 Les Paul Classic begged me to take it home from a motorcycle dealer. It had been traded as collateral on a Harley Davidson. The buyer's wife had said, "Why don't you trade 'em that git-ar you never play?"

The Harley dealer was saddled with the unwanted Gibson. He said, "If you're willing to take it, we just need to turn it into cash."

I said, "Well, gosh, I'd be happy to help!"

Now if you'll excuse me, after thinking about some of the classic guitars I no longer have, I'm going to go give myself a good talking to.

Songstory Writer Tip: Storyboard your song. (What? You mean plan it out?) Yes. What if you planned out a song before you wrote it? You plan your work schedule, your vacation, your Christmas; why not plan your next song? Seriously. List twenty titles. Pick today's best. Decide on a style. Even plan what type of song you need. (I often pushed myself to write more up-tempo female country.)

Write three choruses to fit your title. Pick the best, not the necessarily the first thing that comes to you. Don't sweat filling in all the lines. Now write five verses. You heard me. Pick the best three, or better yet, cobble together the best lines of five verses. Rewrite your opening line until it jumps off the page. Decide on your bridge; sometimes you don't need one. Make sure your last chorus pops with surprise, or irony—anything but predictability.

If you can plan your songs, you can probably become a good and productive writer. You're on your way to writing songs worth writing.

End Note (Fermata)

There are three sides to every story:
your side, my side, and the truth.
(Robert Evans)

There ain't no good guys. There ain't no bad guys.
There's only you and me and we just disagree.
(Jim Krueger)

HAVE YOU EVER noticed how stories improve with the telling? I know mine do. If yours don't, you should probably stop telling them. My memory is fickle: I can recall conversations from fifty years ago verbatim. So how come I always lose my iPhone?

This is my official disclaimer that these are *my* memories. I don't believe we each have our own "truth." God is the only one with a perfect memory, in spite of His age.

My memories are certainly fallible. I need God's help to speak the truth in love (Ephesians 4:15).

I'm certain that a few of those who are named in these pages will say, "That's not how I remember it." Most will admit that my memory is freakishly comprehensive. I would have videotaped the last fifty years, but where would I keep all the tapes? My garage is full.

It is my hope that *Songstory* will resonate with truth as much as possible, but no warranties are herein expressed or implied. I've endeavored to be forthcoming about my own flaws and not exaggerate those of anyone else. May grace abound.

There's an old guitar player joke: How many guitarists does it take to change a light bulb? The punch line is that there will always be a wanna-be saying, "I could have done better." I've written my story to the best of my abilities. Now it gets released into the buzzing marketplace and will be subject to the small minds (and large vocabularies) of anonymous armchair critics. I fall back upon Isaiah 54:17: "No weapon that is fashioned against you shall succeed, and you shall refute every tongue that rises against you in judgment. This is the heritage of the servants of the Lord and their vindication from me, declares the Lord."

So there.

May God bless the readers of this little effort. I have been humbled and amazed at how far my songs have traveled. May the glory of God reflected in these pages shine upon you. Those readers who have read the entirety of this book deserve a reward of some sort. But I don't have one. Perhaps I can take a few of you to coffee. Until then, let us rise for the Benediction:*

---

* Or bend for the rise of diction.

May the Gospel of Christ revolutionize your
   thinking.
May the grace of Christ rule your behavior.
May the presence of Christ restore your soul.

Amen.

Last Songstory Tip: Musicians—spend more time practicing than trying out new equipment. Songwriters—
spend more time considering whether a song idea
is worth writing and less time completing mediocre
thoughts. Thus endeth the sermon.

Thanks for the Memories

Strictly entre nous—Darling, how are you?
And how are all those little dreams
that never did come true?
Awfully glad I met you: Cheerio and tootle-loo.
Thank you. Thank you, so much!
(From "Thanks for the Memory"
by Ralph Rainger and Leo Robin)

HEARTFELT THANKS TO: My beautiful beloved Lori. Crystal, Randall, Sarah, and their families. Thomas and Prater families. The Cotton clans. Best Man Steve Latanation. The Chapmans, Hodges, Scotts, Duncans, Thomson families.

Bob and Jacque. Lees and Mercers, Westminster (PCA) in Fort Myers, First Presbyterian Church in Bonita Springs, Alter Ego horn band, Creative Sound Solutions, Christ Community Church and Parish Presbyterian Church in Franklin, Tennessee.

David Fletcher, Gillette Doggett, Tom Stipe, Greg Laurie, Vince Neypes, Scotty Smith, Nate Larkin, George Grant, Bob Brunson, Byron West. Jeffry Parker, the Songstory book coach. Patti Cotton, life coach. Lori again, for valuable critique. Those supporters of Sweet Comfort Band, ALLIES, Butterfly Kisses, Dolly and Shania, wherever Songstory finds you.

Those mentioned herein who await us in Christ on another shore (Hebrews 12:1).

Bob-bep-poo.

For more information and free Songstory writer tips, please visit randythomasmedia.com.

Sunrise
Randy Thomas, Steve Latanation, John Smaha,
Michael Hodge, Joel Madden
San Bernardino, 1973
Photo Courtesy of Joel Madden.

Sunrise
Randy Thomas, Joel Madden, Steve Latanation, Michael
Hodge, John Smaha.
San Bernardino, 1973
Photo Courtesy of Cherie Roberts.

Psalm150
Joel Madden, Randy Thomas, Greg Eckler, Sam Scott,
Alan Gregory, David Romero.
Huntington Beach, 1975.
Photo Courtesy of Greg Eckler.

Sweet Comfort Band
Rick Thomson, Bryan Duncan, Randy Thomas, Kevin
Thomson.
Backstage, Somewhere, 1979.
Photo Courtesy of Robin Thomson.

ALLIES- The pigeon bomb photo.
Randy Thomas, Bob Carlisle, Sam Scott.
Hollywood, 1984.
Photo Courtesy of Gary Whitlock.

Randy Thomas, Dolly Parton, Bob Carlisle.
San Diego, 1987.
Photo Courtesy of Ray Ware.

Shania Twain, Randy Thomas.
London, 1996.
Photo Courtesy of Sherry Thorn.

Randy and Lori Thomas
Fort Myers, 2017.
Photo Courtesy of Sarah Thomas.

CPSIA information can be obtained
at www.ICGtesting.com
Printed in the USA
FSHW012054041121